# Building My Marriage Before It Begins

## By Dr. Ken Wackes

CORAL RIDGE
MINISTRIES

Published in Ft. Lauderdale, Florida, by Coral Ridge Ministries.

ISBN 1-929626-16-9

Printed in the United States of America.

Scriptures in this book, unless otherwise noted, are from
*The Holy Bible, New International Version* (NIV)
© 1973, 1978, 1984 by International Bible Society,
used by permission of Zondervan Publishing House

# TABLE OF CONTENTS

# INTRODUCTION

It has been said that there are more requirements to getting a driver's license than to get a marriage license. It is also pretty accurate to say that people generally get more instruction in preparing for their driver's license than they do for marriage. However, the damage that can be done by two people poorly prepared for marriage is far greater and has more far reaching consequences than driving a car poorly.

This course is intended to help you form ideas and to make decisions for your future marriage. Rather than just letting marriage "happen" as many people do, I want to help you to make important decisions about your future marriage so that you will go into it informed and equipped to do it well.

You will discover that good marriages do not "just happen." Good, healthy marriages are the result of insight, knowledge, commitment, and hard work. Whatever your marriage becomes in the long run will be either by design (hard decisions and commitments made beforehand and during marriage) or default (slipping and sliding into whatever happens).

You will also discover that God is the creator of marriage. He brought the first man and woman together and continues to bring godly men and women together today. As the creator of marriage, God has given us a manual to be followed—the Bible. In it are many principles for marriage and parenting. Those who learn these principles and live by them are blessed. Those who do not are cursed with

1

unhappiness, pain, and emptiness-the results of not having received blessing. Will you and your marriage be blessed? You determine that.

That is why it is so important now in your life to think about, to think through, and then to commit yourself to God's way.

Many people get married without a clue concerning the divine plan for marriage. Some marry because it is the "proper" thing to do. Others do so with romantic pictures in their minds of "living happily ever after." It is a fantasy world for them. The Scriptures, however, give us at least five major goals that God has in mind for every marriage. By these every marriage will be measured.

The five goals for marriage will be discussed more completely in Chapter Two, but I am listing them here so you can keep then in mind throughout your study. It would be best to simply memorize them now, and plan to adopt them for your future marriage. That is why the title of the course is *Building My Marriage Before It Begins*.

## THE FIVE GOALS OF MARRIAGE

### 1. PROVIDING COMPANIONSHIP FOR EACH OTHER.

The LORD God said, "It is not good for the man to be alone. I will make a helper suitable for him." Now the LORD God had formed out of the ground all the beasts of the field and all the birds of the air. He brought them to the man to see what he would name them; and whatever the man called each living creature, that was its name. So the man gave names to all the livestock, the birds of the air and all the beasts of the field. But for Adam no suitable helper was found. So the LORD God caused the man to fall into a deep sleep; and while he was sleeping, he took one of the man's ribs and closed up the place with flesh. Then the LORD God made a woman from the rib he had taken out of the man, and he brought her to the man.

—*Genesis 2:18-22.*

## 2. SERVING AS INSTRUMENTS IN GOD'S HANDS FOR THE SPIRITUAL GROWTH OF EACH OTHER.

Husbands, love your wives, just as Christ loved the church and gave himself up for her to make her holy, cleansing her by the washing with water through the word, and to present her to himself as a radiant church, without stain or wrinkle or any other blemish, but holy and blameless. In this same way, husbands ought to love their wives as their own bodies. He who loves his wife loves himself.

*—Ephesians 5:25-28.*

## 3. RAISING GODLY CHILDREN TOGETHER TO SERVE GOD IN THE NEXT GENERATION.

Fathers, do not exasperate your children; instead, bring them up in the training and instruction of the Lord.

*—Ephesians 6:4*

Train a child in the way he should go, and when he is old he will not turn from it.

*—Proverbs 22:6*

## 4. WORKING AS PARTNERS IN GOD'S SERVICE.

. . . . the LORD is acting as the witness between you and the wife of your youth, because you have broken faith with her, though she is your partner, the wife of your marriage covenant. Has not [the LORD] made them one? In flesh and spirit they are his. And why one? Because he was seeking godly offspring. So guard yourself in your spirit, and do not break faith with the wife of your youth.

*—Malachi 2:14-15*

## 5. LIVING TOGETHER IN LOVE AND HUMILITY AS A PICTURE OR EXAMPLE OF GOD'S LOVE FOR US.

Husbands, love your wives, just as Christ loved the church and gave himself up for her. . . . "For this reason a man will leave his father and mother and be united to his wife, and the two will become one flesh." This is a profound mystery—but I am talking about Christ and the church. However, each one of you also must love his wife as he loves himself, and the wife must respect her husband.

*—Ephesians 5:25, 31-33*

# Chapter 1

# EIGHT MARRIAGE PATTERNS

## INTRODUCTION

We generally get more instruction in preparing for our driver's license than we do for marriage. To get a driver's license one has to study a book, learn the rules of the road, learn how to interpret roadway signs, maneuver a car safely, and then actually drive the car with an examiner in the front seat. Nothing like that is required to obtain a marriage license. However, the damage that can be done by two people poorly prepared for marriage is far greater and has more far reaching consequences than driving a car poorly.

This course is intended to instruct you about marriage and, to help you form ideas and make decisions for your future marriage. Rather than just letting marriage "happen," as many people do, I want to help you to make important decisions about your future marriage so that you will go into it informed and properly equipped to do it well.

## NOT ALL MARRIAGES ARE THE SAME

The first thing to be understood is the fact that not all marriages are the same. Not everyone drives a car the same way and not every couple conducts their marriage the same way. The goal of this lesson is to help you to deliberately decide what kind of marriage you want to establish. A marriage pattern will emerge very quickly after your wedding day. The question is: Will it be determined by *default* (whatever happens, happens) or by design (choosing a specific plan)?

For example, if you wish to buy a new Corvette, you have several options from which to choose: What size engine? What kind of transmission—stick shift or automatic? What color? Hardtop or convertible? But suppose there were other conditions you were not aware of when you went to the Corvette dealership to pick your car? Outwardly they might all look the same as they sit in the showroom, but inwardly there might be major differences. Over here is a black convertible, but it has no engine. Next to it is a white hardtop, but there is no transmission. The yellow hardtop over there has a faulty electrical system. The green car has no floor board. The red convertible is missing a radiator, and the gray hardtop has no oil pan. The yellow convertible has everything you normally would expect a Corvette to have. Which one will you choose? The yellow convertible, of course! But suppose you are not aware of the limitations of most of these Corvettes? Suppose the only information you have is that they are all called "Corvettes"?

That's the way it is with marriage. Most people think that marriage is marriage is marriage. Some don't last very long; some last a long time, but not happily; some are great experiences; and some are the worst experience the two people have ever had. What's the difference?

## EIGHT MARRIAGE PATTERNS

In American culture there are at least eight marriage patterns that people employ in marriage. From the outside they all look the same, just like the Corvettes. But inside they are as radically different as the car options we looked at. These eight marriage patterns are found among Christians and non-Christians alike. Just because a couple are professing Christians does not automatically mean that their marriage has all of the necessary components to make it work well. Missionaries and pastors often have as unhealthy a marriage pattern as the worst pagan in organized crime.

Your mother and father's marriage has followed one of these eight patterns. What marriage pattern have your parents chosen? What marriage pattern has the person you desire to marry grown up in? More importantly, which pattern for marriage do you want to choose? Will it be determined by default or by design?

- **Pursuing / Passive**
  One of the partners in this marriage pattern entered it with high hopes for a deep, intimate friendship. The other partner soon evidenced a certain lack of interest, energy, and willingness to work at the relationship. The pursuing partner, anticipating what might happen if only he or she works at it harder, increases the pursuit, seeking to pull out of the other partner more enthusiasm for the relationship. Meanwhile, the harder the pursuer pursues, the more distant and apathetic the other partner becomes. The pursuing partner usually takes one of several ultimate paths: to keep on pursuing with increasing vigor until shrillness and a nagging attitude develop; to resign himself or herself to the inevitable ("This is all it will ever be!"); or to become angry, bitter, and walk away from the relationship.

- **Pursuing / Preoccupied**
  Similar to the first marriage pattern described above, one of the partners entered the marriage with high hopes for a deep, intimate friendship. The other partner soon evidenced a certain lack of interest or focus on the marriage relationship. However, in contrast to the passive partner described above, this partner has tons of energy and enthusiasm. Unfortunately, all of his or her energies are directed outside the marriage to other objects of attention—work, hobbies, friendships, church activities, and/or social organizations. The pursuing

partner, anticipating what might happen if only he or she works at it harder, adopts the role of increasing pursuit, seeking to pull the other back into the relationship. However, the more pursuit the pursuer employs, the more distant and seemingly preoccupied the other becomes. As with the Pursuing/Passive marriage, the pursuing partner takes one of several ultimate paths: to keep on pursuing with increasing vigor until shrillness and a nagging attitude develop; to resign himself or herself to the fact that "This is all it will ever be;" or to become angry, bitter, and to walk away from the relationship.

- **Doctor / Patient**
  One of the partners in this marriage pattern evidences deep needs arising from physical or emotional illness, addiction to chemicals or alcohol, or deeply skewed patterns of behavior learned in his or her family of origin. Because of the behaviors arising from whatever condition is at work in this man or woman, the other person in the marriage adopts a caregiver role. As such, he or she makes excuses, covers up, or makes major concessions for the ill partner. When family or friends ask questions, the "doctor" makes up all sorts of alibis for the "patient." When work is missed, the "doctor" lies for the "patient," making up stories about illnesses and injuries that never occurred. It develops into a marriage relationship based upon lies, cover ups, and a cloak of secrecy.

- **Adolescent / Adolescent**
  Psychologists tell us that many people never mature emotionally beyond adolescence (13-15 years of age). As a result, self-control is poorly developed. Selfish behavior often controls the thinking and speaking. "Me," "my," and "mine" are the themes of immaturity. The Adolescent/Adolescent marriage has two immature persons participating in it. What would a marriage look like if the two spouses were both perpetually thirteen or fourteen years old? Imagine the temper tantrums, the fighting and bickering, the petty arguing and insisting on one's own way! That is what this marriage pattern looks like. Soon the two cannot confine their selfish attitudes to the home. Their immaturity spills over into restaurants while dinning with other couples, jumps out at parent-teacher conferences at the children's school,

and erupts while riding in a car on vacation with the kids in the back seat, or while shopping at the local mall. Not a pretty sight!

- **Actor / Actress**
  Often this pattern develops out of the Pursuing/Passive, Pursuing/Preoccupied, or the Adolescent/Adolescent marriage. The two partners simply give up any hope for a healthy, happy relationship and go their separate ways. Because of family values, the need to keep their reputation high at church or in the community, divorce is not an option. They simply become two strangers living in the same house. In public they take on the roles of happily married persons, as an actor or actress would on stage-talking, laughing, sitting together at church or at dinner-but when they shut the front door behind them at home, silence reigns. Some go on separate vacations, maintain separate checking accounts, have two totally different sets of friends and, in general, live apart emotionally, spiritually, and physically.

- **Boss / Employee**
  Whether arising from patterns learned in the family of origin, from a heightened dominance need due to personality type, or out of deep fears of being controlled by another, one of the marriage partners in the Boss/Employee marriage pattern is dominant, controlling, and domineering. The other spouse becomes compliant and obedient. Often the male is the "boss." Some women erroneously think this is the biblical pattern ("Wives, submit to your husbands as to the Lord"). Some men have the same viewpoint ("The husband is the head of the wife, as Christ is the head of the church"). In other situations it is the wife who assumes the role of "boss." She saw her mother do it that way and it seems to fit for her, too! The relationship is one of conquer and be conquered, dominate and be docile, control and be compliant. As with the other marriage patterns listed above, this pattern dehumanizes the two participants and denies their intrinsic worth as bearers of the image of God.

## • Child-Centered

The goal of marriage is a deep relationship of love, sharing, and commitment with a disciplined focus upon the other person and his or her needs and desires. These dynamics are the central core of a healthy marriage. For Christians, a mutual commitment to Christ and obedience to biblical principles on a personal level supply the energy and direction for the relationship. In the Child-Centered marriage, something or someone other than one's spouse becomes the object of attention and focus. Often it is a child. The child serves as the superglue that gives the marriage purpose. The marriage spends its energies on a mutual focus upon the child, rather than upon each other. Take the child out of the picture and nothing remains. When the child leaves home, the glue vanishes and the marriage loses focus. In some marriages it is a pet dog, a farm, a house or garden, a family business, church activity or ministry, a mutual hobby or interest, or, for some, a mutual striving to set aside a sufficient nest egg for retirement that serves as the glue. No matter what serves as the glue, this marriage pattern never provides for the two participants the joy, friendship, and intimacy that God intends for marriage. Any focus that blocks out the biblical instruction to focus on the needs and interests of one's spouse (Ephesians 5:24-25; 1 Peter 3:7) is an illegitimate substitute for the real thing.

## • Committed / Committed

The Committed/Committed marriage pattern is engaged in by two emotionally and spiritually mature persons who are secure enough in Christ and in their sense of self-worth to give themselves to the other person without fear of rejection or loss of identity. To give oneself to another is risky business. It requires a willingness to be vulnerable that only mature persons can give. As we shall see later in these studies, marriage is a sacred covenant sealed by sacred vows of commitment. The commitment is verbalized in the vows taken and lived out daily in the marriage. Although times arise when the couple might resemble persons in one of the other unhealthy patterns, it is only temporary. They always snap back to their underlying relationship of commitment. It is commitment to

Christ, commitment to their vows, commitment personally to each other for a lifetime of faithfulness and mutual support, commitment to intimacy, and commitment to a focus on the other person's needs, and interests. Nothing else is allowed to become central—not children, not work, not church life, not house or garden, not hobbies, not preparations for the future—nothing else but each other under a mutual commitment to Christ. It is a commitment to serve Christ by being used by Him to bring the other person to ever-increasing Christlikeness (Ephesians 5:25-27; 1 Peter 3:1, 7).

Therefore, when we talk about getting ready for marriage, we have to talk about *what kind of marriage* we are getting ourselves ready for, and whether it will be determined by *default or design*?

## ONLY ONE HEALTHY MARRIAGE PATTERN

Only one of the marriage patterns is healthy. Only one allows a marriage couple to live out their marriage in a way described for us in the Bible. Only one frees up both marriage partners to enjoy their marriage to the hilt and receive God's blessing. Of the eight marriage patterns most commonly found in American culture, only one functions in a way that allows the presence of Christ to fill and to expand the relationship. *Of the eight, which would you think to be the healthy marriage pattern?* Committed/committed

The only healthy marriage pattern is the Committed/Committed marriage. But here's the problem—only about 25 percent of all marriages follow the Committed/Committed pattern! If this is the case, no matter where you look around, whether at the local mall or in the local church, the majority of marriages are experiencing less than God intends for them to be. The majority are participating in marriage patterns that inhibit and stunt personal growth, fulfillment, and mutual intimacy. You can be different! You can do it the better way! But you will have to plan to do so for it to happen.

## BY DEFAULT OR DESIGN?

The marriage pattern that comes into existence the day after your marriage ceremony will be *either by default or by design*. If by default, you will stumble into patterns, behaviors, and attitudes that are less than God intends. If your goals and intentions for marriage are different than the ideas brought by your marriage partner, you will be heading for big problems.

Marriage is like a room with two doors leading into it. In one door comes the new husband with a suitcase in each hand. In the other door comes the new wife with a suitcase in each hand. In the suitcases are not clothes, shoes, tennis rackets, silverware, books, or computers. In those suitcases are ideas, values, perceptions, goals, attitudes, practices and habits learned from the partners' family of origin, either without thought or scrutiny or through deliberate and careful planning. How will these two newlyweds live together? That's the big question! Will it be by *default* or by *design*? To not decide is to decide.

The better course of action is to learn the key elements of a godly Committed/Committed marriage, to discuss them together, to pray about them, to discuss them with parents and godly counselors, to write them down, and to adopt them as goals for your marriage. To agree on what your marriage is to be and what to do is an essential step in building your marriage before it starts.

The choices you make about your marriage are to be shaped and determined by what is taught about marriage in the Scriptures. God created marriage. He best knows how to shape and operate it.


## THE BIG IDEAS OF THIS CHAPTER:

1. All marriages follow a specific pattern.
2. Eight general marriage patterns exist in American culture.
3. Only one of the patterns is healthy. Only one of the patterns allows a man and woman to live out their marriage in the way taught in the Scriptures.

4. Only one allows the two to enjoy marriage to the hilt and receive God's full blessing.
5. Christian marriages fall into the same general patterns as do non-Christian marriages.
6. Your marriage will adopt a pattern, either by default or by design.

## QUESTIONS FOR THOUGHT AND DISCUSSION

- In your own words describe a marriage from each of the eight marriage patterns.

- What would it be like to find yourself in one of the unhealthy patterns? Choose one of the unhealthy patterns and let your imagination take you ten years into the future. You are married with one child, and you find yourself in the pattern that you have selected.
  - Describe several elements in the marriage that are not going well.
  - Describe the feelings/emotions you are experiencing in the marriage.
  - What emotions is your spouse experiencing?
  - How do you go about making decisions and resolving conflicts? Be specific as you describe the situations that have emerged in the marriage.
  - Is the marriage relationship what you had hoped it would be prior to marriage?
  - Are you happy and content in the marriage?
  - What are you going to do about it in order to bring improvement to the relationship?

- Do you recognize any marriages around you that seem to fall into one of these patterns? Can you identify one for each pattern?

- Which marriage pattern does the marriage of your parents seem to follow? Write down four or five items that lead you to your conclusion.

- What positive ideas about marriage are you picking up from your parent's marriage? Be specific. Identify items that you want to perpetuate in your own future marriage.

- Compare each of the marriage patterns in the light of what seems to be the picture of marriage painted in Ephesians 5:21-33. How does each compare? What attitudes and behaviors would be present in each that would tend to block the picture from being realized?

- What behaviors will you have to cultivate and develop within yourself if you are going to be a person living happily in a Committed/Committed marriage pattern? Be specific. List at least ten personal behaviors that will be necessary.

- How many of these personal behaviors are present in your life right now? Name them. Which ones are either missing or are not as strong as you would like them to be? Name them.

- What personal behaviors will the person you marry have to possess to be your effective partner in your Committed/Committed marriage? Name them.

- How will you be able to tell if those desired personal behaviors are in the person you are growing to love? What aspects of their life should you observe? How would spending time with them in their parents' home be helpful?

## FURTHER INSIGHTS INTO THE EIGHT MARRIAGE PATTERNS

### PURSUING / PASSIVE

- Wife is usually the committed, pursuing partner; she enters marriage with high hopes for deep friendship.

- Husband usually not aware of wife's basic emotional and spiritual needs· Wife typically has three basic emotional needs: Affection, Security, Intimacy—passive husband fails to meet these needs, is unaware of them, and wife attempts to pull him in her direction. The more she pursues, the more he goes passive and retreats into himself.

- Husband may have come from family in which mother was the leader and father was passive.

- Husband might have a personality that is not naturally assertive and aggressive; if married to a more assertive person, he can become resistant and increasingly more passive.

- What is needed:
  - Husband can benefit from learning about his God-given responsibilities in meeting the deep emotional and spiritual needs of his wife—the major purpose for entering marriage!
  - Husband can benefit from insight received from counseling, books, seminars, etc.
  - It is better if a wife commits her husband and marriage to the Lord rather than attempting to drag out of him what he does not freely give to her. Committing him to God in prayer works in the longer run much better than becoming strident and angry. See Peter's comments in 1 Peter 3:1-6 and his wisdom concerning patience.

## PURSUING / PREOCCUPIED.

- Has several features in common with PURSUING/PASSIVE:
  - Wife is usually committed, pursuing partner.
  - Wife's important emotional and spiritual needs are not met by husband.
  - Husband fails to fulfill God's expectations for him as emotional and spiritual leader in the marriage.

- Preoccupied partner is not passive, but usually very verbal, assertive, capable, achieving, and outwardly competent.

- Chooses for some reason to place his energies elsewhere — work, hobbies, friends, church, etc.

- Possible causes:
  - Old angers against mother/father that are now inappropriately directed against wife.
  - Selfishness, misplaced priorities—work, friends, etc., is placed above wife, family.
  - Husband must reprioritize responsibilities assigned by Lord to be priest and initiator in meeting wife's needs.
  - A pastor or Godly male friend may have to confront him.
  - Husband would be helped through insight from counseling, books, seminars, etc. In committing this to the Lord, wife can learn to be patient and watch God do the difficult thing. Cajoling will not produce what he does not freely give her.

## DOCTOR (NURSE)/PATIENT

- Often one partner has pathological disorder, is addicted to a drug, alcohol, or enmeshed in a set of unhealthy emotional patterns. Not able to carry out responsible adult roles, the "patient" allows the other to cover for them, make excuses, and bear many of their responsibilities.

- Can at times develop suddenly when a spouse becomes depressed and is unable to function normally.

## ADOLESCENT / ADOLESCENT

- A marriage of: (1) two immature persons, or (2) highly selfish persons who live their selfishness out in conflict. Neither is mature enough to save the situation.

- Often married when young for passionate reasons rather than for mature, prepared commitment.

- Could result from two spoiled, "little star" marriage partners who have not learned to share the stage.

- Could develop between two older people who marry after their patterns are virtually set in concrete.

## ACTOR / ACTRESS

- Often caused when anger and bitterness is allowed to build between the two marriage partners. They never learn how to talk out their anger and resolve it. They grow apart in frustration, anger and resentment.

- Walls build that they do not know how to overcome.

- Can result when one of the partners has committed adultery or has otherwise proven to be unfaithful or disloyal. The wronged partner does not want the further pain of divorce. The two simply live in the same house but have a wall of hostility between them. They practice cool civility.

- Couple gives a good show to the outside world when in public and/or to both sides of their families, but within the marriage they simply share the same house. Some couples resort to separate bedrooms, separate vacations and bank accounts, and do not enter at all into the ministry of meeting each others' spiritual and emotional needs.

## BOSS / EMPLOYEE

- Could be a selfish, assertive "My way!" husband or wife.

- Often raised in similar family setting; follows father's/mother's example, even subconsciously seeking a marriage partner like "good old Dad" or "good old Mom."

- Can be caused by one spouse possessing greater abilities and education than wife or husband, or coming from family of origin with greater resources/riches.

- Usually married to inappropriately submissive spouse who allows husband or wife to dominate.

- A husband who fails to understand role as lover, priest, or wife who does not respect her husband as instructed by the Lord (See Ephesians 5:21)

## CHILD-CENTERED

- An object other than one's spouse becomes the focal point of attention and the object for placing affection, time, and energy. In most instances the object of focus and affection is a child. The child's welfare, development, and activities become the center of attention and the glue that holds the household together.

- In some cases it is a pet (pedigreed dogs, show horses), a mutually shared activity, or a mutual hobby (bowling, tennis, boating) that serves as the focal point.

- When the object of attention leaves through marriage (if a child) or old age (if a hobby or activity) the couple often slides into the ACTOR/ACTRESS pattern.

## COMMITTED / COMMITTED

- Usually results from good prior knowledge of roles and responsibilities, gained either through reading and counseling or through a healthy marriage in the family of origin.

- Requires a prior and ongoing commitment to carrying out godly roles and responsibilities.

- Requires a prior and ongoing commitment to the marriage above every other relationship or responsibility. Requires two fairly emotionally healthy partners who are freed from constantly having their own needs met in order to be able to meet the needs of the other.

- Good patterns of interaction, listening, confronting, and conflict resolution are practiced.

- Intimacy becomes a priority, even over the demands and requirements of children.

## A BIBLICAL STUDY

Answer the following interpretive questions from your reading of Ephesians 5:21-31. As you read, keep in mind the eight marriage patterns. Which of the eight seems to be best described in this passage? Which patterns are clearly illegitimate for a Christian couple? By doing this biblical study you are taking steps towards building your marriage before it begins rather than simply allowing it to develop by default.

1. What specific action is found in verse 25? What example is given to be followed? To what extent is this action to be carried out, according to verse 25?
2. According to verses 26 and 27, for what purpose did Christ give Himself up for the Church? What do you think this means? Try to describe it in your own words. See 1 Thessalonians 5:23, John 17:19 and 1 John 1:9.
3. What is the instrument mentioned in verse 26 that Christ uses in this regard?
4. To what specific items mentioned in the previous verses does the phrase "in this same way" refer when describing the function of the husband in relation to his wife?
5. According to verses 26-27, what is one of the primary reasons a man should marry? What is his task? What is the instrument he is to use in this regard? What is his function in the life of his wife?
6. Notice that the ancient words taken from Genesis 2, *"For this reason a man will leave his father and mother and be united to his wife,"* actually are used by Paul in this passage to refer to the matter of intensive, selfless love on the part of a husband for his wife and the task of striving to see that his wife becomes more and more a pure, godly woman. This is quite a bit different than the reasons our society gives for marriage and the function of a husband, isn't it?
7. What is the major verb used in this passage to describe the primary role or responsibility of the Christian wife in her marriage?

8. What example is given as the example she is to follow in this? To what extent is she to do this?

9. What is the primary motivation given in this passage for the woman to keep in mind as she lives this way with her husband?

10. What attitudes and behaviors are suggested in this passage that, if followed, would certainly determine the marriage pattern of the couple? What marriage pattern of the eight best fits the description of God' s plan for marriage as described in this passage?

11. Read 1 Peter 3:1-7. What attitudes and behaviors are described in this passage that, if followed, would strongly influence the marriage pattern a couple should establish? List them.

12. Which marriage pattern would probably emerge if this passage were heeded?

# Chapter 2

# SEVEN PRINCIPLES FOR MARRIAGE

## INTRODUCTION

Not everyone in our culture is a big fan of marriage. Some seek to avoid commitment at all costs. Others see marriage as an irrelevant relic left over from the Ice Age. While browsing through the Internet the following statements were discovered:

"Marriage as an institution developed from rape as a practice. Rape, originally defined as abduction, became marriage by capture. Marriage meant the taking was to extend in time, to be not only use of but possession of, or ownership." (*feminist spokesperson*)

> "Yes, marriage is hateful, detestable. A kind of ineffable, sickening disgust seizes my mind when I think of this most despotic, most unrequited fetter which prejudice has forged to confine its energies." (*world-renowned poet*)

> "I think people really marry far too much; it is such a lottery after all, and for a poor woman a very doubtful happiness." (*famous 18th century Queen of England*)

Not too hopeful, according to these attitudes! However, most Christian guys and girls I know plan to marry, and are excited about the prospect of marrying. Furthermore, according to the Scriptures, marriage for most people is the *preferred*, normal decision to make. Marriage is a great thing to look forward to!

However, many people go into marriage filled with great expectations and dreams, only to have them frustrated and shattered over time.

You will remember that in the previous chapter we looked at the importance of making a good decision beforehand concerning which of the eight marriage patterns we will choose for our marriage. We talked about how important it is to have the necessary information in order to make that decision.

Where can a person get that information? Obviously there are books you could read. There are sites on the Internet you can go to. Some universities even offer Ph.D. programs doing research into marriage patterns and family types. Ultimately, however, joy comes only through knowledge of and obedience to the biblical principles given by God for our enjoyment in marriage.

## THE BASIC SOURCE OF INFORMATION WE HAVE, THE MOST RELIABLE AND TRUSTWORTHY, IS THE BIBLE.

Because God created marriage, it is only logical to assume that He has also given to us guidelines and principles by which we are to shape, frame, and carry out our marriage. Recently I bought a new car, and sure enough, right there in the glove compartment was an owner's manual describing the parts of the car, how often to change the oil, what to do generally to keep the car in good repair, and so on.

The same is true with God and marriage. He has left us with an owner's manual.

After all, God created marriage. It is not the product of social evolution or cultural adaptation. Because God created marriage, it is only logical to assume that He has also given us guidelines and principles by which we are to shape, frame, and carry out our marriage. He has left us with the Owner's manual for the care and upkeep of a healthy marriage. In that manual are principles that are clear and are intended for our good. If we follow them, happiness and joy will result.

## SEVEN PRINCIPLES FOR MARRIAGE

**1. Marriage is God's singular method of uniting a man and a woman as one flesh—spiritually, emotionally, and physically by God's grace.**

Man and woman were intended for intimacy, not aloneness. Marriage is the institution God created to meet this need for intimacy. The human race has invented many possible other ways for people to unite, other than together in sacred marriage. Even married couples have sought substitutes rather than finding this intimacy in their relationship with their own marriage partner. Work, children, activities, even church have been used as substitutes for the real thing.

God has given to the animal kingdom all sorts of arrangements. These pairings have been woven into instincts for breeding and for the survival of the species rather than for intimacy. Humans, however, have been created in the image of God (and not simply a higher form of animal life, as atheistic evolution maintains!), and God has given us a unique institution—marriage—to bring us to completion.

Unfortunately, in our sinfulness, we have attempted to imitate the animals and their instinctual patterns. We live in a culture that promotes and glorifies human alley cats and breeding cattle! In imitation of the animals, mankind has attempted every conceivable arrangement other than God's way. Mankind has contrived numerous counterfeits for the real thing.

There are one-night stands, many coming from meetings at bars that exist for that primary purpose, to pick up or to be picked up. There are other one-time dating events where often the two do not even know each other at all, or only casually.

There are also sexual relationships within a dating relationship where the two persons think that their "dating commitment" is sufficient reason to begin a sexual relationship.

There are people who live together without any binding commitments. A recent news release indicates that there are four million unmarried couples living together in the United States, an increase of one million couples in the last ten years.

*According to Scripture, any sexual relationship outside of marriage is sinful, not allowed, and is contrary to God's law. Why? Because God has built into us an absolute principle for monogamy such that when it is broken, a person inwardly breaks and becomes less than what God intended for him or her to be. This principle is so profound and basic to our nature, that to break it is to experience lifelong consequences.*

Marriage is not a casual relationship of convenience. It is not two people coming together with the idea of living separate lives with different goals, aspirations, plans, as though they were merely sharing a motel room, or playing house for awhile, or on a trial basis to see how it works out. Marriage is becoming one flesh, one mind, one heart, not only in our commitment to each other, but in our desire to please, to serve, and to glorify God.

## 2. Marriage is mutual commitment to a lifetime covenant, sealed by a sacred oath.

Marriage for a lifetime is what most people still anticipate and hope for. And it is what most people who marry still experience. One husband and one wife for a lifetime. But for this to really work with joy and lifelong friendship and happiness takes personal commitment.

Marriage is not an easily broken contract. It is not a short-term proposition to remain married as long as we feel like it. In God's plan, marriage is for keeps. Without deep commitment for a lifetime, it simply will not work.

We live in a society where commitment is not a widely held virtue. I see students dropping classes when it gets too hard; athletes dropping off teams when they do not get enough playing time; people in the work force that break contracts when a better offer comes from another company; people in churches who volunteer for a committee and pledge to do their tasks, but who never do; and couples who pledge to live with each other in marriage for a lifetime, but who turn around a few years later only to glare at each other in divorce court. Divorce is not an option for Christians. Divorce is the admission that a couple has been unable or unwilling to trust the same God who raised Jesus from the dead to resurrect their marriage. Divorce, except in instances clearly stated in Scripture (*See Matthew 5:31-32; Matthew 19:3-6; and, 1 Corinthians 7:10-16. See also Malachi 2:13-16*) is never an option for believers in Christ.

Marriage is a covenant (see Malachi 2:13-16) in which two become one flesh, one mind, and one heart by oath, invoking God as their witness. The marriage oath says two things. First, it is voluntarily stating that we are willing to have God deal with us if we break that oath. Second, it states that we are opening ourselves up to receive God's blessing, grace, desire, ability, and power to become what He wants us to be in our marriage, as we trust Him and yield to each other. What God requires, He supplies as we depend upon Him!

Before you marry, the question is, will you commit yourself to this other person for a lifetime, without exception? Will you seal that commitment before God by means of a sacred oath?

### 3. The marriage covenant is to be monogamous.

I once lived in a culture that practiced polygamy. I knew many men who had two or more wives. It was a status symbol in that culture, a sign of wealth and prestige. When I returned to America I discovered that a new form of polygamy was gaining in popularity. Although polygamy is officially outlawed in the United States, it is very common now for many people to practice what some refer to as "serial polygamy." That is, a man or a woman who has, through marriage and divorce, had multiple marriage partners during their lifetime—but only one at a time. God's principle has established that marriage is to *one,* person for a lifetime.

The divine principle from the beginning was one man and one woman in a covenant relationship for the duration of their earthly life. The first marriage God created was monogamous, involving two who become one, not three who become one, or one who becomes two with two others simultaneously.

The ideal standard for godly men is found in the New Testament: "Now the overseer must be above reproach, the husband of but one wife, temperate, self-controlled, respectable, hospitable, able to teach," (1 Timothy 3:2); "A deacon must be the husband of but one wife and must manage his children and his household well" (1Timothy 3:12).

## 4. The marriage covenant is permissible and possible only with another Christian.

When the Apostle Paul brought the Gospel of Jesus Christ to the Greek city of Corinth, there was a lot of confusion about marriage. Corinth was a seaport filled with sailors and prostitutes. Corinth was also devoted to the worship of Diana, the goddess of sensuality and sex. Young men and women were expected to serve as sacred prostitutes in the temple for a period of time before they married and set up their families. There was bound to be confusion among the new Christians.

In his two letters to the Christians at Corinth the Apostle Paul made two important statements about whom Christians are free to marry. First, "A woman is bound to her husband as long as he lives. But if her husband dies, she is free to marry anyone she wishes, *but he must belong to the Lord*" (1 Corinthians 7:39). Some women were already married when they became Christians. Were they really married in God's sight? Certainly, said the Apostle. In fact, they were so much married in God's sight that Paul said, "If a woman has a husband who is not a believer and he is willing to live with her, she must not divorce him" (1 Corinthians 7:13). However, he said, if her first husband dies, she is free to remarry, *but he must belong to the Lord*. His second teaching is even clearer than the first. "Do not be yoked together with unbelievers. For what do righteousness and wickedness have in common? Or what fellowship can light have with darkness? What harmony is there between Christ and Belial? What does a believer have in common with an unbeliever? What agreement is there between the temple of God and idols? For we are the temple of the living God. As God has said: 'I will live with them and walk among them, and I will be their God, and they will be my people.' 'Therefore come out from them and be separate, says the Lord. Touch no unclean thing, and I will receive you.' 'I will be a Father to you, and you will be my sons and daughters, says the Lord Almighty'" (2 Corinthians 6:14-18).

### 5. The marriage covenant is a relationship containing specific biblical roles and responsibilities.

There is great confusion in our culture about how two people are to go about this business of marriage. Feminists generally argue against marriage, stating that it is a relationship of slavery for the woman, on the one hand, or else a relationship with a male who lives a very selfish, self-centered life, on the other. Who needs that, they argue? And you know what, if that's all marriage is, I would agree! This confusion about marriage has resulted in a deep confusion about what roles people are to carry out in marriage. Many who have studied the breakdown of marriage in America state that a major cause of the breakdown is role confusion. The debate goes on and on. Are there roles based upon gender? Are roles in marriage based upon ability and preference? Are there any specific roles at all? Again, God comes to the rescue and lays out for us very clearly how roles and responsibilities are to be carried out in marriage, and by whom.

The roles in marriage are most clearly set out for us in Ephesians 5:21-33 and will be examined more closely in a later chapter.

### 6. The marriage covenant is a partnership in God's service.

Is marriage only for establishing a life-long friendship? Is it for the rearing of children? What is the ultimate goal for marriage? Marriage is intended to create a partnership of two Christians who love each other deeply, but who also are deeply devoted together to serving God as a team. The Cultural Mandate given to Adam and Eve, as recorded in Genesis 1:28, was the first commissioning for service, as it were, by God for marriage. That mandate still stands for all marriages to fulfill. We are never certain about where God will lead us to live, or what He will lead us to do, or to what ministry He will urge us to devote ourselves, but one thing we must determine to do through our marriages and that is to serve God together with all of our heart, mind, soul, and strength.

### 7. The marriage covenant is God's method for producing Christlikeness in the husband and wife through mutual help and upbuilding.

This is the most important of all the principles contained in the Bible concerning marriage.

The basis for this principle is the apostle Paul's admonition in Ephesians 5:21, "Submit to one another out of reverence for Christ." He goes on to speak specifically to the husband, teaching him that he is to give himself up for the purpose of perfecting holiness, purity, and godliness in his wife, as Christ does for the Church. That is why he is called to be the husband in her life.

When I counsel couples prior to marriage, I ask each to think about a very important truth. God's goal for us, from the moment we place our faith in Jesus until the day we die physically, is to ever increasingly reproduce Jesus within us—so that we more and more take on the thoughts and attitudes and behaviors of Jesus Christ. God uses the Bible, the Church, friends, trials, and all sorts of other means to do this. But marriage is crucial to this process as well. When I marry a woman I am to understand that God intends to use me, her husband, as a priest in her life to perfect Christ in her. And when I marry her, this means that out of all the Christian men in the world God could use for this purpose, He has chosen me! And out of all the Christian women He could use to perfect Christ in me, He chose my wife.

That's heavy! That's an awesome thought! But it is true. Marriage is serious stuff. It is about Christ, about God, about helping each other to grow more and more into the likeness of Jesus. It is not about having our own needs met. It is not about getting our own way. It is not about even being happy all the time with the person we marry. It is about being a tool in God's hands to form Christ in my wife or my husband. That is why I can only think about marriage in relationship with another Christian who has the maturity and the love for God to participate with me in this adventure.

## THE PURPOSE FOR THESE PRINCIPLES

The purpose for these principles is not to confine us, to hurt us, or to make marriage a rigid set of codes, but rather to free us up to enjoy and to be deeply satisfied in and through our marriage. God's way always works, it is always the best way, and it is always the *only* way to true blessing, happiness, and joy. The Creator of the object always knows best for what reasons he designed it and how it is to be used and enjoyed. Married Christians will either be blessed of God because of their commitment to biblical principles governing marriage or they will be devoid of God's blessing. The marriage you are preparing for will either be blessed or not blessed. It might function well with relative peace and happiness, but the deep, satisfying, unifying blessing of God will be absent if His Word and His ways are ignored.

## THE BIG IDEAS OF THIS CHAPTER:

1. Marriage is God's creation. It is his idea. He brings Christian men and women together for a lifetime relationship.
2. God has given to us at least seven principles in the Bible by which we are to shape and govern our marriages.
3. We live in a culture where many people are either ignorant about or simply ignore those principles.
4. Christian marriage is mutual commitment within a covenant, sealed by a sacred vow.
5. Obedience to these principles brings blessing. Disobedience brings pain, disappointment, and frustration.
6. We can only carry out these principles when married to another committed, faithful Christian.
7. When I marry another person, I am acknowledging that God has selected me to be the one person from among all other persons on earth to be an instrument in His hands to produce Christlikeness in the person I marry.

## QUESTION FOR THOUGHT
## AND DISCUSSION

1. What would some say is the difference between living together in a college dorm outside of marriage and engaging in sexual behavior together in a dating relationship? Would their arguments be valid? Why or why not? Which of these two scenarios is a healthy preparation for marriage? Explain your answer.

2. Christian counselors indicate that often when counseling troubled married couples, they have learned to ask about the sexual relationship the two had prior to marriage. Why do you suppose this is the case? What bearing might sexual relationships *prior* to marriage have on troubles *within* a marriage?

3. What do the following biblical passages teach about the various alternates to God's way for male/female relationships devised by mankind? *Galatians 5:19; Ephesians 5:3, 11, 12; I Thessalonians 4:3.* What are some of the inevitable consequences of rejecting God's principle of practicing sexual love only within the boundaries of a life-long commitment in marriage? *I Corinthians 6:9-18; Ephesians 5:5-6; Hebrews 13:4; Psalm 38:1-10* (This is David's own account of his sexual sin's payback-a payback that is inevitable for the Christian who is disobedient.)

4. If marriage is a mutual commitment to a covenant that is sealed by a sacred oath, what do the following biblical passages add to the current idea that marriage, rather than being a covenant, is an easily broken contract? *1 Corinthians 7:12-14, 39-40; Matthew 19:4-6; Malachi 2:14-16; Mark 10:5; Matthew 5:31-32.*

5. There are times when a particular person loses his or her right to remain married due to personal sin (*Matthew 5:31-32*). However, what does God advocate as higher principles for a marriage in trouble, rather than divorce? *II Corinthians 9:8; 12:9; Ephesians 4:7; Hebrews 4:16; James 4:6; II Peter 3:18.*

6. If there is hope of forgiveness for something like divorce, why not disobey God when the going gets tough in marriage, and then simply ask him to forgive me after it's over? (What possi-

ble attitudes would such a comment reveal, according to John 14:23-24 and I John 3:24?)

7. What are some of the arrangements you have observed in life or through the media that men and women have used to coordinate their roles and responsibilities in marriage? Try to discuss several that are in contrast to each other. After you have done this, read Ephesians 5:21-33 and then 1 Peter 3:1-8.

8. What do the two apostles teach about roles and responsibilities in marriage? Who or what is the great standard against which we are to measure ourselves as married people, whether female or male, wife or husband? What are the key verbs used to describe our marital roles and responsibilities?

9. Go back and observe principles six and seven. Note that one is outward in focus and the other inward. One brings together two people into a union and bond for the purpose of serving God together for a lifetime. The other focuses on each other. In your own words, what does principle seven really mean? How does it fly smack in the face of the numerous reasons people give as an excuse for divorce? For more insight into this matter, read carefully James 1. What are trials? Why are they intended? Where do they come from? Who stands behind, over, under, and around them for our good? What is the connection between disputes, disagreements, ways of doing things differently than we are used to, gender-related differences that can be aggravating, etc., and trials mentioned in James 1?

## ADDED NOTES FOR READING AND DISCUSSION

Many who have studied the breakdown of marriage in America state that a major cause of the breakdown is role confusion. Are there any roles based upon gender? Are roles in marriage merely based upon ability and preference, skills, or personality traits? Are there any assigned roles at all? Again, God comes to the rescue and lays out for us very clearly how the marriage relationship has been designed to avoid chaos and confusion. A deep reading and study of Ephesians 5, not one that is shallow and flippant, will open truth to this important issue.

Marriage is not only for establishing a deep friendship, or for the rearing of children. Marriage for Christians involves two people who also are deeply devoted together to serving God as a team. They never are certain about where God will lead them to live, or what He will lead them to do, or to what kind of ministry He will urge them to devote themselves, or for how long. But one thing they have determined: They will serve God together with all of their heart, mind, soul, and strength.

When the apostle Paul states in Ephesians 5:21, "Submit to one another out of reverence for Christ," he goes on to speak specifically to the husband, teaching him that he is to give himself up, as Christ did, for the purpose of seeing holiness, purity, and godliness develop in his wife. That is why he is called to be the husband in her life. From the moment we place our faith in Jesus, until the day we die physically, Christ works to ever increasingly reproduce Himself in us—so that we more and more take on His thoughts, attitudes, and behaviors. He uses the Bible, the Church, friends, and trials to do this. But marriage is important to this as well. When a man marries, he assumes the responsibility from God to serve as a priest in her life. Out of all the Christian men in the world that God could use for this purpose, he has been chosen for her specifically! And out of all the Christian women that He could use to perfect Christ in that man, He chose his wife to be that woman! No principle for marriage is more important than this one.

That is an awesome thought! But it is true. Marriage is serious stuff. It is about Christ, about God, about helping each other to grow more and more into the likeness of Jesus. It's not about having our own needs met. It is not about getting our own way. It is not about even being happy all the time with the person we marry. It is about being committed to a relationship and a covenant. It is being a tool in God's hands to form Christ in my wife or my husband. That is why we can only think about marriage in relationship with another Christian, one who has personally embraced Christ as Lord and Savior. No one else can enter with us into the marriage covenant with God's blessing.

# Chapter 3

# SEVEN MAJOR
# FAMILY TYPES

## INTRODUCTION

Once, when I was about eleven or twelve years old, I was invited to go to a friend's house after school to play and to eat supper. No one was home when we got there. No one showed up all afternoon. When dinnertime came my friend headed for the kitchen and opening the refrigerator asked, "What would you like to eat?" Tuna fish? Hot dogs? Peanut butter and jelly?" We settled on hot dogs and ate them, just the two of us, at the kitchen table. During the meal his mother came home with food for herself in a bag and sat down with us to eat. Later on his father came home, stating that he had eaten on the way home, and went out into the garage to work on his car. "Do you always eat like this," I asked him? "Yeah. Most of the time," he said.

That was the first time I realized that not every family operated like mine. I later met people who lived in all different kinds of families from the one I was raised in.

Virtually all families belong to one or two of seven dominant family patterns that exist in American culture.

## MARRIAGE PATTERNS DETERMINE FAMILY TYPES

The pattern that a family develops is determined by the marriage relationship of the parents. *The marriage pattern determines the family type.* The marriage pattern established, either by default or design, creates a specific family type. That family type becomes the environment for the children born into that family.

We previously examined the eight marriage patterns that exist in American culture. We also saw that all marriages take on their particular pattern by either default or by design—and so will yours. Of the eight dominant marriage patterns, only one is healthy—the Committed/Committed marriage pattern.

In this chapter we will examine the relationship between the marriage pattern you select for your marriage and the family type that tends to emerge from that marriage pattern. There is a principle that holds true all the time: *every marriage sets the tone for and creates a particular family type.*

Back to the story about eating dinner at my friend's house—you could probably come up with several very accurate, educated statements about the pattern of marriage being experienced by his mother and father. That night as we ate hot dogs at the kitchen table, and then with the arrival of his mother, and later his father, that scene spoke volumes about their marriage pattern. The marriage pattern established either by default or design, in turn creates a specific family type.

In American culture there are at least seven major family types.

## SEVEN MAJOR FAMILY TYPES IN AMERICAN CULTURE

### 1. The ENMESHED Family

In the enmeshed family the parents live their lives through their children, allowing little opportunity for the child to stand on his own, think his own thoughts, act independently apart from the parent's goals, dreams, and plans established for the child. The parents attempt to live their dreams, ambitions, and often what they personally failed to achieve themselves in their childhood and youth through their children's activities. "You are a traitor if you act independently of us or seek to live your life apart from us." They live like several octopi, all interlocked and indistinguishable from one another. Marriage of their child or children presents a major problem for this family. They worry how can they possibly survive if the child leaves the nest. Often marrying into such a family presents a real problem for the in-law newcomer. Do they get sucked into the relationship? Should they fight to help their spouse break free from the tentacles of the home? If they do, what will the outcome be? Should the new groom go into business with his father-in-law, which is what the enmeshed family desires? Should the newlyweds live with her parents, move next door to them, or eat dinner with them almost daily? Pretty soon the lines become blurred. Who is married to whom? What role in the new marriage does the husband of the enmeshed daughter carry out? Is he a new son who now also is enmeshed? Is he viewed as an outsider attempting to rob the enmeshed family of a daughter?

## 2. The LITTLE STAR Family

The basic motivation in this family pattern is the advancement and promotion of the child, who, set out as if on a stage, becomes the life and breath of the family. "My time, my resources, my life, have only one goal, and that is promoting you to the top place in whatever activity you find yourself in," is the message. Only positive messages and only successes are allowed. There is no allowance here for negative consequences from which to learn. The child is led to believe that he or she is the greatest, capable of anything. There is little, if any, realistic assessment of, or teaching about, gifts, abilities, talents, limitations, or choosing to occupy the place of "the least among the saints." All obstacles to achieving the established goals, including other people, are attacked with fervor. Only gold stamps are issued. The existence of things negative is denied. "You are the greatest above all others!"

3. The MOTHER HEN Family

In this family pattern, mother and father shield the child from negative elements in life by using protective devices and fences that keep the negative elements of life away from the child. The goal is to keep out all negative circumstances and consequences with a firm refusal to allow the child to learn through natural and/or imposed consequences. "I don't want you to learn the hard way like I did! I don't want you to go through the tough times I experienced, " is the message. Parents within the Mother Hen family pattern often do maintain a form of discipline at home, requiring courtesy and obedience to the expectations of the home. But no one from the outside and no authority other than the parent is ever allowed to deal negatively with the child. Schoolteachers, youth league coaches, and parents of other children in the neighborhood are often viewed as the enemy whenever they attempt to require the child to conform to their expectations or deal with the child when he or she does not. The family sets up clear fences between "us" and "them." "We will never allow anything bad to happen to you," is the underlying theme of this family pattern.

4. The CONNECTING Family

The Connecting Family best produces emotional and spiritual health in the child. The important elements necessary for healthy emotional development in the child, godliness, individuality, and connectivity, are found in rich abundance with relative equal emphasis. Present is a balanced blending of all the items required for healthy growth. Strong bonding is characteristic of the interactions and relationships in this family pattern. Intimacy is experienced between family members; connectivity is experienced as a major feature; there is an ongoing open dialogue intergenerationally with parents and grandparents, and the same between siblings. Rules and expectations are present in healthy amounts. Consequences are allowed to teach. The family is viewed as the developing ground for strong husbands and wives of the next generation. Thus, the parents' marriage relationship takes priority over everything else taking place in the family. Love is given out continually, in large measures, and always unconditionally. "You are accountable for your behavior here, and you are also loved here unconditionally," is the underlying message.

## 5. The ADMIRAL OF THE SHIP Family

Rules and compliance with the rules tend to take priority over relationships in this family pattern. While love may be present, the subtle message that underlies everything is, "Performance counts!" "You fit in here to the degree you conform to the rules and expectations," is the message. Often the family shields the child through excessive fences that limit the range of the child in decision-making, risk taking, and choosing between alternatives. Rules tend to confine individuality. Requirements and expectations tend to limit the ability to think issues through and to discourage the ability to weigh and choose between alternatives "You're accepted here if you perform to our expectations. If you don't, you're not." Usually one parent serves as Admiral of the Ship, with the other serving as First Mate.

## 6. The BROWN STAMPS Family

Nothing pleases the judge or meets the expectations in this family pattern. Criticism, judging motives and actions, and passing out negative rewards seem to be at the heart of the relationships in this family pattern. Whether dealing with each other within the family, or dealing with those without, negative criticism is the primary dynamic. Every day is like a courtroom; all actions and achievements are on trial; nothing earns respect or reward; no achievement is ever good enough; no praise or positive input received; no gold stamps are received, only negative brown stamps. "Try as you might, but your best is never good enough."

## 7. The LAISSEZ-FAIRE Family

Chaos and lack of connectedness marks this family pattern. Every one in the family looks out for himself, with little interaction with the rest of the family. Little attention is given to the rearing of the children. The Laissez-Faire pattern can result from preoccupation on the part of the parents with their own lives and with their own activities and interests. In some instances it is the result of overwhelming financial problems, physical health problems, chemical addictions, or neurosis. In some instances it results from a believed philosophy of parenting: "I won't do anything that alienates me from being my child's friend, not even disciplining or setting rules. I'd rather be his friend than his mother or father." The basic message learned by the children in this family pattern is "Every man for himself in this family. Survive if you can."

## BASIC MESSAGES CONVEYED BY THE SEVEN FAMILY TYPES:

**Enmeshed:** "We are one. I live my life through you. You are my purpose and meaning in life. If you leave or vary from my plan for you, you are a traitor." (Stifling)

**Little Star:** "You are simply the world's greatest, and all of life revolves around you. I will promote you with all the energy and resources I have. You can do no wrong." (Promoting)

**Mother Hen:** "I won't let anything bad happen to you. Protecting you means not allowing negative consequences to ever be experienced by you from the outside." (Protecting)

**Admiral of the Ship:** "Rules and performance are important here. You are accepted if you keep the rules and not accepted if you don't. Your worth is based upon your performance." (Ruling)

**Connecting:** "Rules and performance are important. But so are you. We love you and accept you unconditionally. Our relationship is just as important as what we do and require." (Balance)

**Brown Stamps:** "You never do anything right! You are not capable and therefore not loved." (Criticizing)

**Laissez-Faire:** "Everybody survives on his own; everyone looks out for himself around here." (Ignoring)

## THE BIG IDEAS OF THIS CHAPTER:

1. Not all families operate the same way.
2. There are at least seven family types in American culture.
3. Only the Connected Family Type provides health for the children and the parents.
4. Only the Connected Family Type provides the proper balance between Individuality and Connectivity, the two elements necessary for healthy child development.
5. The family type that will result from your marriage will depend upon the particular marriage pattern you establish by design.
6. The Connected Family Type only results from the Committed/Committed Marriage Pattern.

## QUESTIONS FOR THOUGHT AND DISCUSSION

1. In which Family Type were you raised? (Some ask if it could be a combination of several patterns. In some instances several patterns could be at work at the same time. It depends on who is home and who is in charge at the moment, whether dad or mom.)
2. Do you think a particular family could change its pattern over time? If so, what would be some dynamics that would tend to impact the family towards change, either negatively or positively?
3. See if you can visualize families you know that fit these Family Types. Visualize one for each type. Let them dance around in your thoughts for a while. What do you notice are the major differences between the families you visualized? Be specific. Name at least three differences between them.
4. To say that the Family Type in which I was born had a great impact on how well I have developed as a person sounds pretty deterministic to some: "I am who and what I am be-

cause of my family." Do you agree or disagree? Why, or why not?

5. How can information like the data you are thinking about right now assist a person to move beyond what has been developed through their Family of Origin (a term for the family in which you were born and raised)?

6. Which of the Family Types do you think can function effectively in passing on the truth about God and Jesus Christ to the children of the family? Which one(s) would not be very effective, and why?

7. Is the Family Type an important issue in determining whom you should date? Would their Family Type influence their ability to be a healthy, balanced marriage partner?

8. Which Family Type would you like to form as an outgrowth of your Marriage Pattern?

9. How might Family Types lend to the development of (1) sexual promiscuity; (2) a wall flower; (3) a thief; (4) a chameleon; (5) a brat; (6) a liar; (7) a well-adjusted kid?

10. Describe the dynamics and features of the Connected Family. Unless you are clear about this, you will not tend to be able to develop such a family when it is your turn to form a household.

**An added dimension to the impact of the family pattern on the development of children:**

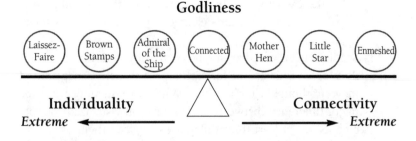

All children need rich resources from their family environment in order to develop into healthy persons. The major dynamics of

*Godliness, Individuality,* and *Connectivity* are crucial and must be developed in such a way as to ensure balance in the developing child. Spiritually and emotionally healthy adults are balanced to the degree that these three elements are balanced in their lives. The goal of the spiritually minded family is to see these elements developed in their children and to shape their families to that end.

*Individuality* must be contrasted with individualism. *Individualism* is a centering upon self, often to the exclusion of others and their needs. Individuality is identifying and learning to use the specifically unique gifts, traits, and abilities that make each person an individual. Each person bears God's fingerprints in a unique way. Individuality is the ability to stand alone in a healthy way without excluding the worth, dignity, and needs of others and without feeling compelled to take on the characteristics of another person. Children who develop without this important element often live life as chameleons, changing this way and that, depending upon whom they are associated with at any given moment. On the other hand, children with heightened individuality, without a balancing of connectivity, develop self-reliant individualism without proper regard for others. Thus, a healthy balance is crucially important.

*Connectivity* is the desire for and the ability to live well with other people, to relate healthily to those people without losing one's own uniqueness, dignity, and worth.

## FAMILY PATTERNS AND SPIRITUAL DEVELOPMENT

Each of the seven Family Types moves in one direction or the other. Each moves towards an extreme. The further along the *Individuality* line one goes, the less well developed he or she is in *Connectivity*. The further along the *Connectivity* line one goes, the less well developed he or she is in *Individuality*. Much of that depends on the family in which the person is raised. The Enmeshed Family develops *Connectivity* to a sick, inappropriate degree, and to the virtual absence of *Individuality*. The Laissez-Faire Family develops *Individuality* to a sick, inappropriate degree, and to the virtual absence of *Connectivity*.

Children who develop in family patterns along the extreme ends of the spectrum will have a difficult time living in a healthy relationship with God. Their perspective on things spiritual will tend to reflect the perspective gained from their family pattern.

The child of the Enmeshed Family will struggle with many doctrinal issues, including the ability to stand-alone for the Christian faith and identifying and activating the spiritual gifts given by God to the child for kingdom service. Leaving mother and father for the sake of the kingdom will be a very difficult task, on the one hand, as will be leaving father and mother to become one flesh with his or her spouse.

The child of the Laissez-Faire Family will struggle with issues of trust, faith, and reliance upon God and His power. The lifelong pattern of "I have to do it on my own" will conflict with the necessity of relying upon Jesus Christ alone for salvation and upon the Spirit of God for growth in the Christian life.

Children raised in the Brown Stamp Family will often become bitter and resistant to the Christian faith if parents who continually criticize and fault-find are seen as standard-bearers for true Christianity. "If that is a reflection of God," a youth will conclude, "then I want nothing to do with that kind of God."

Likewise, the Little Star will become so enamored with his or her own importance that the need for a Savior will not be apparent.

Therefore, determining to build a healthy family before it begins is a spiritual activity of the utmost importance.

# Chapter 4

# TRUSTING GOD FOR MY MARRIAGE PARTNER

## INTRODUCTION

"Will I get married or not?" That is a question that many people ask themselves prior to finding their life's marriage partner. Some, observing the poor marriage of their own parents, have had such a bad experience at home that they know one thing: If that is what marriage is like, they want nothing to do with it. Others, having experienced the divorce of their parents, fear marriage. But most people I know look forward to marriage. They have always just assumed that they will get married.

It's one thing to look at the eight marriage patterns, understand the seven principles for marriage, and be able to identify seven family types, but you have a deeper issue you need to resolve: Will you get married or not?

## KEY QUESTIONS TO BE ASKED:
- Will I marry or not?
- If I do, to whom?
- Where will I meet that person?
- Where are they right now?

- When is this going to happen?
- How will I know when I meet the right person?
- Does God select someone for me, or is it all up to me?

## GOD'S PRIMARY OBJECTIVE IN OUR LIVES:

God has something much more important on his mind than if we marry or not. His primary objective is to form Christ in us (Romans 8:28-30). He wants us to more and more resemble Jesus Christ in the way we think and talk, and we behave, the way we view God and ourselves, and the way we perceive life and its circumstances. That is God's goal for each of us. We will never be completed projects in this earthly life. We perfectly resemble Jesus only when we enter Heaven in His presence. But meanwhile, back here on earth, day-by-day, week-by-week, God is slowly shaping and molding us into Christlikeness.

There are two things about us that are primary. Nothing else comes even close in importance to these two goals in God's eyes.

▲ God's *will* being achieved in us and through us.
▲ Christ's *character* being formed in us.

Normally it is God's intention for people to marry. We can conclude this from the creation story of Adam and Eve where we are told that God saw that it is not good for a man or a woman to be alone. God also gave to humanity the mandate to be fruitful and multiply. The apostle Paul noted that it was better for most people to marry. He also described the ideal leader in the local church as a man who is married to one wife. The writer of Hebrews stated that marriage is to be honored by all.

In some instances, however, it is *not* God's will for a person to marry. Some people are led by God to *forego* marriage in order to serve him in a special way, or to go to a part of the world in his service where it would place great strain on a marriage. We also know that some people living very normal lives in very normal places are called by God to remain unmarried for reasons known only to God.

That is why the issue is not really whether or not I marry. Rather,

the issue is, *how will Christ best be formed in me?* Will He use the MAR-
RIED state or the UNMARRIED state? And will it be the married state
for a while and then through death of my spouse the single state
again? What is God's design for my life?

## GOD ALONE HAS THE RIGHT TO MAKE
## THE CHOICE FOR US.

As a Christian I am to leave that matter to God and to walk by
faith and obedience as I watch Him work in my life day-by-day and
year-by-year. Everything else, including whether or not I marry, and
if so, to whom, will fall into place. He knows what is best. He has already laid out the plan for us. To yield to God's will in this matter is
what marks a true follower of Christ.

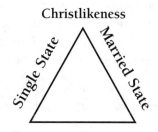

**God's method for forming
Christ in me**

## FIVE KEY AREAS OF YIELDING:

1. I will yield to God, at the core of my life and above all else,
   that the character of CHRIST will be formed in me.

   I want that to be the driving force in my life, in all that I do, in all decisions that I make, in all paths that I follow for the rest of my life.
   That is what is involved when the writer of Proverbs says, "Trust in
   the LORD with all your heart and lean not on your own understanding; in all your ways acknowledge him, and he will make your paths

straight" (Proverbs 3:5, 6). Paul wrote to the new Christians in Europe, addressing them in his letter as, "My dear children, for whom I am again in the pains of childbirth until *Christ is formed in you . . ."* (Galatians 4:19). You can take this to the bank. It is an absolute certainty. *Nothing in all of life is more important and central than for you to have Christ formed in you.*

Having made that decision, three other areas of yielding follow right behind:

2. I will subordinate the issue of whether I MARRY or DO NOT MARRY to the higher issue of having Christ formed in me.

Will I marry or not? Some Christians are bitter and angry about not being married. Some worry and are anxious. They fear that they are getting older and are still not married. Getting married becomes the overriding issue of their lives. Their primary concern is getting married, not having the character of Christ formed within. They have failed to relate marriage to the will of God for their lives.

The spiritual person comes to the issue with the firm resolve that he or she will *yield to the Lord the issue of whether to marry or not marry.*

3. I will yield the matter of WHOM I marry to the Lord.

The person with whom I will live for the rest of my life is not my choice to make, primarily, but God's. I will trust Him to do that. I do not know how He will let me know who it is. I do not know where I will be when He does it. I do not know how old I will be. I do not know who that person is. But I will trust God to do that for me. He will let me know in His own way.

If I leave the matter of selecting my marriage partner to the Lord, obviously He is going to choose someone for me who will meet His standards. It will be a person who is:

• A growing Christian who will be my PARTNER in God's service.

- Emotionally and spiritually mature enough to be God's IN-STRUMENT to help form Christ in me.
- FREE to marry me (i.e., they are not married to someone else, nor have they been divorced from someone else in a manner that is not allowed in Scripture).
- A growing Christian of the opposite gender. (Sorry, we have to say that, even though it is clear in Scripture. Our present culture is so confused, it has to be repeated.)

I have watched some people jump ahead of God. Rather than waiting for His choice, they have impatiently jumped into *hasty marriages* that are flawed from the start. Others have jumped into marriages that had no basis other than *physical attraction* and a physical relationship that soon soured. Some have married *non-Christians*, thinking that a non-Christian spouse is better than no spouse at all, or that they can "change" the person after marriage. Some have married people who, because of previous experiences with marriage, *are not eligible* in God's eyes to marry again. Others have jumped into an *"I don't need your advice!"* marriage, when their parents or friends tried to caution them against a marriage that seemed ill advised. Tragedy and heartbreak are the result.

4. I will seek the Lord's guidance through my parents, seeking their PERMISSION and BLESSING.

It has been widely noted that the culture in which everyone else is excluded from the decision about selecting one's marriage partner is the culture with the highest divorce rate. The covenant concept of marriage, common courtesy, respect, and the collective wisdom of those who raised us, dictate the involvement of our parents.

5. I will yield the TIMING of marriage to the Lord.

- Are we both spiritually and emotionally ready to assume such a major responsibility?

- Do we know enough about each other to be absolutely certain that we are the ones we want to parent our children and to be lifelong partners in God's service?
- Are we economically able to undertake marriage? Is there excessive debt that must be taken care of first?
- Are we both practicing sexual self-control in our relationship so that there is a healthy mutual trusting of each other? Are we experiencing God-directed love, or is this simply physical infatuation?

**Important note:** A negative response to any one of the items above might indicate that it is wise to wait awhile until counseling can assist us in resolving the issue(s).

## BIG IDEAS OF THIS CHAPTER:

1. Marriage always has to be viewed in the light of a greater issue: how does God choose to form *Christ* in me?
2. I will yield to God in four other crucial matters:

   (1) I will yield the issue of whether I *will* or *will not* marry to the Lord.
   (2) I will yield to God the right to choose the *person* to whom I will be married.
   (3) I will seek the Lord's guidance through my parents, seeking their *permission* and *blessing*.
   (4) I will yield the *timing* of my marriage to the Lord.

## QUESTIONS FOR FURTHER THOUGHT AND DISCUSSION

1. Have you ever before considered marriage as a means to a greater end: becoming more and more like Jesus Christ? What are your thoughts right now as you let this idea sink into your

inner person? Does it scare you, that perhaps God will seemingly "punish" you by not leading you into marriage?

2. What truth could you bring gently to a friend who continually talks about their frustrations with still being unmarried? (Picture yourself with such a friend in your early thirties. What truth could you gently bring to a friend who laments *being* married? What kind word would be appropriate to help a friend who brags about not wanting to "get tied down?"

3. Do you know anyone who obviously was in a big rush to marry and did not take the time to consider well the emotional and/or spiritual condition of the one they married? What were the results? Is all necessarily lost? Why, or why not?

4. How would you explain the fact that marriage, being a spiritual covenant, involves in some way the blessing and permission of your parents? Is there a difference between having parents who are in a Christian covenant relationship versus those who are not? What might be an appropriate response for a person to make to their parent should they say, "Hey! You're not a little kid anymore! That's a matter for only you to decide."

5. Does Ephesians 6:1-3 have anything to say about how I am to go about choosing my marriage partner? If so, what? If not, why not? Are there any limitations, like age, where I live, or whether I am working or in school in this passage?

6. What do you think about the traditional practice, long since abandoned by many in our culture, of the husband-to-be asking his fiancée's father for his blessing and permission? How might involving parents through their blessing build a stronger and healthier relationship for the couple and with their parents if they carried out this principle? How might the action of not seeking this from parents create hidden, but nonetheless, slighted or bruised feelings, especially within the bride's father?

7. Listen carefully to the warning given above in this chapter that deals with the necessity for the absolute certainty of emotional health and maturity. What is faulty with the following idea: "I

know that he/she has a rough spot at that point in their attitudes and/or behavior, but I am certain that it will go away
after we are married?"

## ADDED MATERIAL FOR READING
## AND DISCUSSION

Read the book, *High Risk: Children Without A Conscience*, by Ken
Magid. Use the checklists in this book to evaluate your own life and
that of the one you are considering marrying.

Read Romans 8:28-29. What does it teach us about yielding the
matter of marriage to the Lord? Does it support or contradict the big
ideas of this chapter? Pray over the passage, specifically yielding the
matter of marriage to the Lord as you do so. Have you ever memo-
rized this passage? If not, it would be a great passage to memorize.

Chapter 5

# IT'S ALL IN YOUR BRAIN!

## INTRODUCTION

Marriages often find themselves in trouble for one simple reason: husbands and wives generally are unaware that *males and females are different!* Someone once said that the difficulty lies in the fact that a woman thinks she is marrying another woman and the man thinks he is marrying another man. What is meant by this observation is that females tend to expect their husbands to think, feel, communicate, and respond as a female would, and males expect their wives to respond like another male.

This is an area about which most people have received little insight and have done little reading. Insight into these differences will enable you to function with more knowledge and with better skills in marriage.

Some would maintain that there are no essential differences between men and women other than those of a mere anatomical nature. Their ideas are not based upon scientific research but grow, rather, out of a personal agenda that would like us to believe that no real differences exist between males and females. Neurological and psychological studies, which we will discuss in this chapter, have shown, however, that many significant differences of an emotional, psychological, physiological, and communication nature do exist between the genders.

To state that real differences exist between the two genders does not infer in any way that one gender is superior or inferior to the other. It is simply to face the fact that we are different! God made us that way. If God made us with significant gender differences, we are foolish and will become very frustrated if we make believe these differences do not exist. We are to identify, acknowledge, and learn to capture these differences for the good of our marriages and families.

## GENDER BY DESIGN!

You are who you are in gender by God's deliberate design. It is not a matter of luck or chance. *Your gender is a gift from God.*

*"So God created man in his own image, in the image of God he created him; male and female he created them. . . . He created them male and female and he blessed them"* (Genesis. 1:27; 5:2).

Both genders are created in God's image. Both carry glory as God's image bearers. There are two genders, not three or four. Both genders are alike in that they bear God's image; both dissimilar in that they are separate genders with separate gender differences; both, however, alike in that they are intended for each other.

To deny one's gender-gift is a rebellion against God. To deny the gender-gift of another person is equally rebellious. To treat with contempt the opposite gender or one with that gender-gift is a sin. As Christians we are to be grateful to God for our gender-gift, to realize that it has been given for a purpose that is pleasing to God, and to seek to glorify God through our gender-gift.

## GENDER DIFFERENCES DO EXIST.

We know from a variety of studies that males are inherently different from females and females inherently different from males. God designed these gender differences. Gender differences go far beyond the differences of physical anatomy or reproductive systems. The differences are almost innumerable, extending from very simple and obvious differences to differences that are at the very depths of our being. To deny them is to deny our gender uniqueness, and to deny our gender uniqueness is to deny the God who gave to us our gender identity.

There are several areas of difference between the female gender and the male gender that are crucially important in their significance.

## PHYSIOLOGICAL DIFFERENCES:

There are many physiological differences between females and males. Some are very obvious. Others are not. The following are a few examples from the hundreds of physiological differences between females and males.

- There are 20 percent fewer red blood cells in a female's blood than a male's. Since these are the trailer trucks of the blood stream that carry their payloads of oxygen throughout the body, a female tends to fatigue more readily from physical exertion than a male.

- The metabolism rate of males is normally greater than females. Males generally burn more energy due to their higher metabolism rate. Thus, males can lose weight faster than females, but they can also put it back on faster than women can!

- The normal resting heartbeat of a female is more rapid than a male's, averaging almost ten beats a minute faster. A female's blood pressure tends to be lower, and females experience high blood pressure problems less frequently than males.

- In their skeletal structure males tend to have a longer body trunk and shorter limbs in proportion to their entire body. As a result, the male is capable of 50% greater body strength on the average than a female of a relatively similar weight and size.

- The female has larger internal organs (liver, appendix, stomach, kidneys). This is God's special design enabling her to care for a little human being within her during pregnancy.

- The male has a larger set of lungs and a greater breathing capacity. When coupled with the difference in the number of red blood cells and skeletal structure, it allows the male to perform with greater strength and with greater endurance than the female in most physically exerting activities.

- The female has several significant bodily processes, each connected to a complicated and unique hormonal makeup, that are absent in the male. Among these are menstruation, pregnancy, and lactation.

- Glandularly, the important thyroid gland in the female is larger and more active. It grows larger and becomes more active during menstruation and pregnancy. This produces a greater resistance to cold temperatures and gives her smoother skin and relatively less body hair. The thyroid becomes more active during menstruation, causing, in many females, headaches, cramps, flare-ups of allergies and asthma, and greater emotional tension.

- Due to estrogens produced, females seem to be shielded against the most common forms of heart disease. Although both genders are afflicted, heart disease is much less frequent for females than for males.

- A higher percentage of males die during birth and infancy than do females. Males have more frequent occurrences of speech, hearing, and learning disorders than do females.

## SUMMARY:

While some may maintain that male and female differences are insignificant, the evidence is overwhelmingly to the contrary. The physiological differences between males and females are legion. They are far more extensive and far-reaching than mere differences in reproductive organs and reproduction-related systems or processes. The differences are real, numerous and affect moods, behaviors, and even physical capacities. This does not mean that one is superior to the other. The issue is not competition. One is not preferred over the other. The point is to simply stand back in wonder at the design evidenced in us that testifies to a wonderful Creator God who knew exactly what He was doing when He designed us.

## BRAIN DIFFERENCES:

During the past twenty years numerous studies have been conducted throughout the world seeking to discover how children learn. Some are visual learners—they have to see it to learn it. Some are auditory learners—they learn best by hearing. Others are kinesthetic—they have to be moving around in order to learn. Some are tactile learners—they learn best when able to touch or try out with their senses something being studied. The goal has been to understand the whole matter of how people learn and by what delivery system the information of life is best processed by their brain.

Similar studies have been conducted with people who have had severe brain injuries through automobile and other traumatizing accidents. Such studies have sought to identify which parts of the brain are in charge of which functions of the physical and neurological systems of the body.

As a result of these studies we now know more about and understand better the psychological makeup of boys and girls. We also have come to understand better not only how the brain functions but also the significant brain differences that exist between males and females.

I live within one hour of two major universities. Both have leading departments that specialize in examining the human brain and the unique ways the male brain functions and the unique ways the female brain functions. (A book listed at the end of this chapter, *Brain Sex*, is an excellent survey of this issue and contains an anthology of many of the brain studies that have been conducted in Europe and the United States.)

## THE BRAIN

What a wonderfully complex organ God designed as the central computer of our earthly, physical body! Some have referred to it as the most complex thing in the whole universe. It is comprised of a trillion cells; 100 billion of them are linked in a series of networks that serve as the basis for intelligence, emotions, consciousness, creativity, and memory.

But that complexity of cells linked together does not alone account for the uniqueness of the human brain. Other organs in the body contain approximately the same number of cells as the brain, but a thousand of them put together do not add up to the wonders of the brain and its functions.

## MEMORY AND VISION

Various parts of the brain are involved in different forms of remembering. Generally speaking, the front of the brain is involved with short-term memory, while the rear portions deal with long-term memory. Cramming for a test involves the front of the brain. Remembering your telephone number, your name, or your birthday are items stored away in the vast filing cabinets of the rear portions of the brain.

A blow to either portion of the brain during a football game or an automobile accident, or damage through a tumor or other ailment can impair the functions of whatever portion of the brain has been damaged. We've all read about persons who just wandered off and could not remember who they were or where they belonged.

A friend of mine had surgery on the left side of his brain due to a tumor that had developed. The results of that surgery have made major changes to his life and to his marriage. Prior to the surgery, he was a computer systems analyst for a national computer manufacturer. He was somewhat introverted and compliant. After the surgery he became increasingly vocal, assertive, and, because his long-term memory was impaired, could no longer work as a systems analyst. His wife was married to a totally different person! I spent many sessions with them in an attempt to identify the dynamics of this new marriage relationship.

My friend returned to university life where he majored in music composition. He now teaches courses in music at the local state university and leads the music program in a local church, all because of surgery on one part of his brain!

In a similar way, a lack of blood supply to the front of the brain due to clogged arteries in an older person can wipe out the short-term memory functions of the brain. In such cases, a person might view as a total stranger the pastor who has been in the church for the last two years, but remembers vividly who the third grade teacher was from fifty years ago!

I stopped my car one morning to assist an old lady wandering down a main street in her pajamas. She had not the foggiest idea where the retirement home was that she entered six months prior, but talked on and on, while seated in my car, about her prior career as a teacher in New York City.

Other portions of the brain control speech. Any damage through disease, accident, or nerve damage can seriously impair speech. This is why a stroke can often result in blurred speech or the loss of speech altogether. When a child has great difficulty learning to talk, the possibility of nerve impairment or damage is often suspected.

## TWO HEMISPHERES

When viewed from the top the brain looks like a walnut in its shell. Weighing about three to four pounds, the brain is divided into distinct parts, with two major sections—the left and right hemispheres—connected by a series of nerve bridges collectively forming the *corpus callosum*.

Research indicates that each of these two hemispheres tends to control different functions. The left hemisphere controls language and speech, for instance, while the right hemisphere processes color, dimensions, and spatial relationships.

Most people tend to "favor" one side of the brain or the other. Some (favoring the left hemisphere) seem naturally attracted to lists, outlines, math problems, logical progressions, and grammar, for instance. They are big on time management and schedules. They are the first to buy the latest organizer on the market. Others, however, (favoring the right hemisphere) seem to lose all track of time in their daily lives, for they get occupied in their favorite things—art, photography, color, drama, dance, music, conversation. People tend to gravitate towards those activities and tendencies belonging to one side or the other. This is referred to as being *left-brain dominant* and *right-brain dominant.*

Some people are dominant in both hemispheres. Others, because of the demands of particular responsibilities they must fulfill, learn to develop functions that do not come naturally to them (right-brain dominant students still must successfully pass math courses, and the left-brain dominant office manager must engage in small talk at the water fountain and send birthday cards to his staff)! This is called compensating. Thus, right-brainers probably would benefit from a time-management course and the left-brainers from a good course in relaxation techniques.

As a person who tends towards right-brain activities, one day my secretary gave me a piece of mail with the comment, "Here! I think you should look at this. It might be helpful!" It was an ad for a weeklong seminar conducted by a time-management company. I took the hint, and it changed my life! I learned techniques and processes linked with left-brained activities and became a better manager. I learned to compensate.

## WHAT DOES THIS HAVE TO DO WITH
## MALE/FEMALE DIFFERENCES?

The major point to be made for the two hemispheres of the brain as it affects male and female differences is found by traveling back in time to the development of the unborn child, especially the male child in his mother's womb. Some researchers have indicated that it is the *corpus callosum* where the differences can be traced. The *corpus callosum* contains millions of nerve bridges that connect one hemisphere of the brain to the other. They are bridges across which all kinds of messages and communications travel.

Some research seems to indicate, although not agreed to by other brain researchers, that during pregnancy when *testosterone*, the male sex hormone, begins to develop in the little male child, it changes the brain in ways unique to the male gender. As it is secreted through the little boy's developing body, which leads to the various male uniquenesses, radical changes in the brain take place. Acting as a kind of acid wash, *testosterone* washes across the little boy's brain, burning away many of the nerve bridges in the *corpus callosum*. This greatly affects the rate and volume of messages that travel from one side of the brain to the other. Fewer nerve bridges mean fewer messages. Alterations take place, these researchers say, that forever change the structure of that little brain. It creates an alteration that forever makes the little boy's brain entirely different from the brain of his mother or sister.

Some researchers have further speculated that in males who are right-brain dominant, the amount of *testosterone* manufactured during the pregnancy may have been less than for a male who is left-brained.

It is this strange occurrence that might be the source of the basis for one of the most profound, confusing, and until recently, little understood differences between males and females. What takes place in his mother's womb when *testosterone* does its work makes a man in his thinking and even in his behavior and communicating very different from his girlfriend or his wife. This might be the cause for many misunderstandings and breakdowns in male-female relationships.

## THE MALE BRAIN

### THE MALE BRAIN FUNCTIONS WITH UNIQUE CHARACTERISTICS.

A male can be either left-brain dominant or right-brain dominant, or even have strengths in both hemispheres. But he will tend to only operate out of one hemisphere at a time. He becomes more focused or one-hemisphere oriented as his brain processes and operates. What this means is that he may be a very talented and gifted individual but he can only concentrate on and do one thing at a time. This lies at the heart of what has confused women about men over the generations—*the compartmentalization of men in their thinking and behavior.*

## THE MALE BRAIN TENDS TO BE COMPARTMENTALIZED.

Countless cartoons have appeared in newspapers and magazines featuring a man sitting in a living room chair reading his paper. His wife thinks she is engaging with him in a meaningful conversation. He responds to her with grunts and "uh-hums" (while he continues to sit reading the sports page of the paper). Soon she realizes that he hasn't heard one word she said! A man, because of his one-side-of-the-brain-at-a-time processing, cannot read the paper and listen to her at the same time.

Thus, the female, if she wants to be certain she has his attention and wants to engage in meaningful conversation with him, must get his undivided attention. This is best achieved by getting his direct eye contact and addressing him face-to-face. Attempting to talk to him from another room in the house while he is reading the paper or watching television is not a productive method.

A woman, on the other hand, because she is usually able to function with both hemispheres at the same time, is more *wholistic* and *inclusive* in her thinking and in her attending to things that go on around her. She can be cleaning the floor in one end of the house, all the while very conscious and alert to a baby's faintest whimpers on the other end of the house.

On the other hand, she will become very frustrated when she leaves her child home for the evening with her husband and leaves careful instructions about bathing the child and reading to him and praying with him before bedtime, only to arrive home at 10 PM with the pots and pans pulled out of the kitchen cabinets, toys all over the floor, and the child still wide awake, still unbathed, and evidently not very well attended to in her absence. What happened? Her husband became preoccupied with his computer or a baseball game on television or an interesting article in the newly arrived computer magazine.

*The male brain tends to be compartmentalized.* Each compartment

has a major focus. Food. Exercise. Hobbies. TV. Work. God. Wife.
Children. Friends. Parents. Sex. Sports. News. Chores. And so on.

| WIFE | WORK | FOOD | SEX |
|--------|--------|------|------|
| SPORTS | | | $$ |
| CHORES | HEALTH | CAR | KIDS |

Because of the way the male brain tends to function, the male
can be fully involved with any of these boxes, but he will be tend to
be able to function in only one box at a time.

This is a fact that causes great confusion for his wife, mother, or
female friend. She often sees him to be one who is preoccupied, not
listening, not caring, not interested.

Male compartmentalization is the cause of a man's reluctance
to talk about his work when he comes home in the evening. "Work
is work. Home is home. Let's not confuse the two." Or why, if he is
honest, the typical man, when asked by his wife, "Did you think
about me today at work?" would have to acknowledge that not
once did it even occur to him to remember that he was married, let
alone give moments of thought to his wife or things pertaining to
her! If he is to call her during the day, he often needs memos or
some other gimmick to remind him to switch gears and give
thought to calling her.

- The male is compartmentalized. He concentrates on one
  thing at a time.

- The female is wholistic. She takes in the whole scenario at
  once.

Men cannot use these differences in the male as excuses. Understanding that they exist is important so he can compensate for them
and better meet the needs of his wife and daughter for communication, sharing, and intimacy. Likewise, his wife and daughter must

understand that these differences exist and be patient as he attempts to compensate.

## COMMON SITUATIONS IN MARRIAGE RESULTING FROM THIS DIFFERENCE

Men are often accused of being closed, non-communicative, non-intimate, and preoccupied. Because intimacy is one of the three basic emotional needs of the woman (together with the need for affection and security), her need for intimacy is often not met when she fails to receive her husband's undivided attention.

The computer, newspaper, and television set are all often viewed as competitors for her husband's attention.

Most things in his life are compartmentalized. He concentrates on one thing at a time.

Because she fails to understand this fundamental male/female difference, she concludes that he does not love her.

The wise woman understands her husband's tendency towards compartmentalization and works to gain his attention, giving him space and rest when needed. She is fortunate if she also is married to a wise man who, understanding his wife's need for intimacy and his own reluctance to provide this at times when he is preoccupied with other things in his life, works hard to overcome his one-thing-at-a-time tendencies.

## THE FEMALE BRAIN

In the majority of females the right side of the brain tends to be dominant. This is not to say that there are not many females who are left-brain dominant. There are, however, the difference is that females are better able to involve both hemispheres of the brain, no matter which hemisphere is dominant in a particular female.

Thus, females tend to be more concerned with the contextual than with the abstract. Studies at Johns Hopkins University suggest that the apparent mathematical advancement of males is not environmental-it is not simply the result of boys being more encouraged to take higher level math courses than female students, but is the result of how the male and the female brains process.

Females tend to be more skilled at verbal and communication skills, thus they are more verbal and communicative. They are more "people" oriented and "socially alert" than they are concerned about things or tasks. They are tuned in to listening for, sensing, and perceiving the verbal communication of others. They are adept at sensing and perceiving the nuances and feelings lying behind the actual words rather than focusing, like the male does, on the literal words being used.

They are more alert to the feelings, emotions, and needs of other people than are males. In several studies the reaction and focus of little girls were compared to little boys when, in a controlled environment, things like sounds, objects, faces, and voices were introduced. Invariably the little girls, when confronted with several objects or sounds competing for their attention, responded to people, faces, and voices rather than to inanimate objects like fire trucks, stuffed animals or balls.

Females are more wholistic, seeing the whole picture and the interrelationships between events, people, and emotions. They have the unique ability to "read between the lines." This ability has been termed "woman's intuition" in our culture.

| KIDS | PARENTS | CHORES | GOD |
|---|---|---|---|
| FOOD | FRIENDS | CHURCH | TV |
| EXERCISE | HOBBY | FRIENDS | HUSBAND |

## COMMON SITUATIONS IN MARRIAGE RESULTING FROM THIS DIFFERENCE

Women tend to seek higher degrees of intimacy and friendship, whereas men tend to share their feelings and ideas less often and less freely. Women often take this characteristic of men to mean secrecy, lack of love, lack of friendship, or lack of commitment to the marriage. Such may not be the case at all.

Her ability to see things wholistically causes the female to make very definite connections between attitudes, behaviors, and tones of voice. Her ability to have a desire for sexual intimacy, for example, is directly tied to the relationship she has with her husband generally and within the immediate timeframe in particular. The man, on the other hand, often makes no connection between events. Whether or not her husband took the garbage out on time and without being reminded, whether he was warm and gentle when he said good-bye on his way to work, whether he telephoned her during the day—all of these things can affect the woman's sexual responsiveness that evening. But her husband is bewildered! He never will understand what taking garbage cans out in the morning has to do with sexual intimacy in the evening!

### ANOTHER FEMALE/MALE BRAIN-RELATED DIFFERENCE

Women tend not to say what they mean. Often deep feelings and sensitivities lie behind the words they choose. Men, however, tend to be concrete and literal. They take words spoken for their face value.

The tendency by males towards literalism can drive a wife to frustration. A woman, after her husband just repeated back to her word for word what he heard her say, often exclaims in frustration, "That's not what I said at all!" What she really means is, "That's not what I *meant*." All of this can be confusing to the husband and frustrating for the wife. It is at this very point that many marital disputes take place.

Because a woman tends to read between the lines and to fill in the spaces (as she thinks they should be filled in), broken communication can take place when she attempts to "read" her husband, who tends to be less communicative in the first place. When he does speak, he doesn't like people to "read between the lines." He believes that he says what he means and means what he says!

Once, a man in passing said to his wife, "The garage looks junky; we need to clean it up." Since the next day was Saturday when those kinds of things were taken care of, she assumed he meant, "Tomorrow, let's clean up the garage." So she quickly finished her own chores around the house on Saturday morning in order to help him clean up the garage. When he finished his chores (cutting the lawn, washing the car) he prepared to go to the store to buy what he needed for another project, fertilizing the shrubs. She became very upset that he was not preparing to attack the garage as he said he would the night before! After all, she reasoned, she had rearranged her whole Saturday to help him in the garage!

What he literally said was, "The garage looks junky; we need to clean it up." What she read this to mean was, "Tomorrow, let's clean up the garage."

## A REVIEW OF MALE/FEMALE DIFFERENCES

| *Male* | *Female* |
|---|---|
| • One thing at a time | • Wholistic thinking |
| • Task oriented | • Relationship oriented |
| • Conquer oriented | • Process oriented |
| • Less sensitive to feelings, emotions and nuances | • Very sensitive to feelings, emotions and nuances |
| • Quest for independence and privacy | • Quest for intimacy and belonging |
| • Less hormonal complexity | • Greater hormonal complexity |
| • Higher adrenaline levels | • Lower adrenaline levels |
| • Higher metabolism rate | • Lower metabolism rate |
| • Concrete, literal | • Reads between the lines |
| • Focus on words spoken | • Focus on feelings implied |

## IMPLICATIONS FOR MARRIAGE:

Both the wife and the husband, different as they are, must become sensitive to the inherent gender qualities and characteristics of the other.

- Husbands must work hard at learning how to move out of their little boxes and into areas of sharing and intimacy in order to meet the need for relationship and intimacy their wives have by divine creation.

- Wives must work hard at learning how to be patient with the compartmentalization of their husbands, to not take the male tendencies for privacy and independence personally, and to not to judge the commitment to their relationship by their husband's male characteristics.

- A wise wife understands her husband's compartmentalization, learns to capture the "right moments," and aims for his undivided attention through eye-to-eye contact.

- A sensitive husband recognizes his compartmentalization and therefore his tendency to not meet his wife's need for intimacy and security through shared relationship. He compensates by learning to move more comfortably from one box to the other, even when he doesn't feel like doing it.

## BIG IDEAS OF THIS CHAPTER:

1. Physiological and brain differences do exist between the two genders.
2. The male tends to be compartmentalized. He concentrates on one thing at a time. The female tends to be wholistic. She is able to take in the whole scenario at once.
3. Males tend to be task oriented, whereas females tend to be relationship oriented.

4. Gender differences can cause major disruptions in a marriage and in the family unless they are understood, responded to with patience, and wisely compensated for.

## QUESTIONS FOR FURTHER THOUGHT AND DISCUSSION

1. How could the television set, the newspaper, and the computer—all inanimate objects without a life of their own—be viewed deeply and emotionally by a woman as competitors for her husband's love and affection?
2. What steps could a wise husband take to reduce his wife's anxiety and feelings of detachment, with regard to the issues dealt with in the above question?
3. Why might a husband be reluctant to go over all the events of the day's work when he walks through the front door in the evening? Cite several possible reasons.
4. Why might a wife be eager to go over all the events of the day at work when she walks through the front door in the evening? Cite several possible reasons.
5. What labels might a husband put on his wife's attempts to ask him questions about his day at work? What are some possible unhealthy responses he might give to her requests for conversation? What are some possible healthy responses he might give?
6. Why might a man be more prone to sharing the events of the day after dinner, after some moments alone for relaxation, or after finishing up several chores around the house?
7. How does our culture show its commonsense understanding of gender differences with its frequent reference to "a woman's intuition" but seldom, if ever, with references to "a man's intuition?"
8. How might a female's natural urge to "read between the lines" cause frustration and bewilderment in her husband, brother, or father?

9. Why is this information crucially important to those preparing themselves for marriage?

FOR FURTHER EXPLORATION:

*Brain Sex*, Anne Moir and David Jessel, New York: Dell Publishing, 1991. (Readings in male/female brain characteristics.)

Using one of the many search engines available, explore the numerous web sites and articles on the Internet that discuss male/female brain differences.

# Chapter 6

# HE SAID, SHE SAID: VERBAL COMMUNICATION DIFFERENCES

## INTRODUCTION

John and Barbara talked on the telephone last night. She could tell that he was preoccupied with studying for a big test the next morning and so their conversation was short. They did make plans to eat lunch together after class the next day since they had not really seen each other for several days. Both attend the same university but have very different schedules on the large campus of 35,000 students. It was Barbara's idea to eat lunch together, and in his usual way, when preoccupied, John agreed with an "Uh-huh." It was all he could do to get that response out, so engrossed was he in studying for the exam. He had fallen behind this semester in this particular course and the exam was especially important.

The next day Barbara waited twenty minutes for him to show. No John. She waited thirty minutes. No John. Finally, she grabbed something to eat quickly at the Student Center and rushed off to her after-noon class. You can imagine the conversation that night when John called to tell her how difficult the exam was that morning, but how good he felt about how he thought he had done!

"Where were you this morning?" she asked.

"Taking my exam. Where do you think I was?" he responded.

"I mean, for lunch," exclaimed Barbara.

"Lunch? I went to get a hamburger with Tom and Fred after the exam. Why?"

John's response was the start of a pretty testy conversation. He strongly denied ever knowing that he was supposed to meet Barbara for lunch. He commented that the whole relationship was *getting to him* because this incident was another in a long line of occasions in which she made up stories about what he supposedly said, but really *didn't*. He expressed his concern about her overly active imagination!

Barbara, on the other hand, was *totally* frustrated. *How can you agree to eat lunch together, and then the very next day deny the conversation ever took place?* "Is John a liar," she asks herself? "Is he crazy?" "Maybe it's a sign that he doesn't really want to be around me or have a relationship with me," she thinks. "I wonder if there is another girl he has met. His old girlfriend who just transferred over from the community college—are they seeing each other again?"

## REVIEW OF BRAIN DIFFERENCES

The misunderstanding between Barbara and John is one that leads us to the main topic of this chapter—female and male communication differences. It is a continuation of our investigating several of the basic male and female differences.

In the last chapter we discovered that males and females are very different in the ways that their brains function. One is highly com-partmentalized, dealing with one thing at a time and appears to be preoccupied because of being stuck in one box of focus. The other is wholistic and able to juggle a number of things at once with con-centration, and able to focus on several boxes at a time. One is less sensitive to feelings, and emotions and is less adept at reading between-the-lines communication. The other is very sensitive to feelings and emotions as well as more adept at reading between-the-lines communication. One tends to be factual and to the point; the other tends to be figurative and takes longer to get to the point—All because of the way their brains function!

There are those who deny these differences. However, increasingly, brain studies are validating much of what we discovered in the last chapter.

*Back to John and Barbara:* Was John trying to avoid Barbara? No. He never even remembered the lunch agreement. He never *heard* it. Was Barbara being unreasonable and delusional? No! The conversation really *did* take place! Is there another girl involved? No! John was merely locked into his little brain box, and Barbara never took the necessary first steps to bring him out of the "study for exam" box. She merely assumed that because they were engaged in a telephone conversation that he was in the box she thought he was in, "We haven't had much time together recently, have we?" Just think what happens in a marriage when these kinds of dialogues happen again and again, month after month, and year after year!

In this chapter we will only deal with how males and females, because of their differences in perceiving life around them, tend to develop conflicting verbal communication patterns that are unique to the two genders.

## VERBAL COMMUNICATION DIFFERENCES

In her widely read book, You Just Don't Understand: Women and Men in Conversation, Dr. Deborah Tannen reveals the radical difference between males and females in their verbal communication patterns, and uncovers the basic gender-developed perceptions of life that are behind these patterns.

TANNEN'S EXPLANATION OF THE BASIC GENDER-DEVELOPED PERCEPTIONS OF LIFE:

- **Males tend to perceive life *vertically* — big issues are "top" and "bottom"**

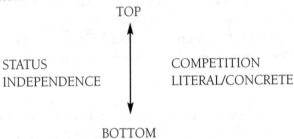

Key terms that characterize the male perception of life:
Top and Bottom, Status, Competition, Independence (freedom from control), and Literal/Concrete Communication.

- **Females tend to perceive life *horizontally*—big issues are "close" and "far"**

*Key terms that characterize the female perception of life:*

*Close and Far, Relationship, Cooperation, Intimacy and Inclusion, and Meta-Messages (Intuitive).*

You can think of all kinds of situations that you have observed between your parents or grandparents, or situations that you have had personally, that now, all of a sudden, start to make a lot of sense!

You know now exactly what was taking place! As a guy, was your mother or your girlfriend trying to compete with you and control your independence? No, probably not. They simply wanted to *know*. Know *what*? The actual facts? Not really. They just wanted to be included in what you were thinking and doing. As a girl, is your father, or brother, or latest boyfriend, when he seems distant and not intimate, really trying to push you away? Is he in a sneaky way trying to tell you that he is not interested in you any more? No, probably not. He's simply in a far away land somewhere on a distant planet, caught up in one of his little brain boxes.

There are times at the dinner table when my wife thinks she is having a good relational conversation with me, when all of a sudden she sees that distant, foggy look in my eyes. I've moved out of the box containing the conversation of the moment to another, usually the box labeled "WORK" or "WHAT I HAVE TO GET DONE TONIGHT." Waving her hands at the other side of the table, she says, "Earth to space, come in Ken!" and with a chuckle we resume the conversation.

Males tend to focus on one box at a time. They can start out in one box at the beginning of a conversation, but drift off into another, more pressing box. They tend to be "one-thing-at-a-time" creatures for whose attention mothers, girlfriends; and wives have to work hard to obtain (*and keep!*). On the other hand, a male can become very confused by the mother, girlfriend, or wife who seems to start out in one box, suddenly slide over into another box, and jump into a third box, all within one series of comments! To her wholistic mind, it all makes sense. But the one-box-at-a-time male she is talking to is trying to figure out what in the world is going on!

## BOYS AND GIRLS AT PLAY

Dr. Tannen states that observing little boys and girls as they play further illustrates these differences. Even their play patterns, the specific kinds of games they play, and where they play them reflect these two fundamentally different ways of perceiving life.

Little boys like to play in larger groups. They tend to be loud, pushy, boastful, and extremely competitive; bragging about who can do what better, arguing over rules, and wrestling for recognition and status. They tend to play outdoors. A lot of energy is consumed. Their conversations are about "stuff." Who is better than whom? Who is tougher, bigger, and stronger than whom? They aren't really all that concerned with who gets to play (as long as they are included), who gets a turn to participate (as long as they get their turn, and as many turns as possible!), and who gets left out. At times the game never begins because they never get past the big issue of who chooses the teams, who gets chosen first, and who takes the first turn at bat, gets possession of the basketball, or goes on offense with the football. When the teams are chosen they fight over who gets to pitch, who is the quarterback, or who takes the most shots. Even after they get into the game, the game is often disrupted and even scuttled by arguments over who fouled whom, who was out of bounds, and who makes the final decision about such disagreements! Often it ends in shouting and pushing, or they simply disband, leaving behind a trail of mocking words and put-downs.

Little girls, on the other hand, tend to play in smaller groups or in pairs. Rather than intense competition, they tend to focus on cooperation—everyone gets a turn—they form intimacy-based relationships where secrets, and "just-me-and-you" items are shared. They are often content to just sit and talk. When they get older the telephone is a passion!

| Boys | Girls |
|---|---|
| • Tend to play outside | • Tend to play inside |
| • Play in large groups | • Play in small groups or pairs |
| • Hierarchically structured relationships | • Intimacy-based relationships |
| • Leaders tell others what to do | • Everyone gets a turn to play |
| • Giving orders and making sure they are followed | • Expressing ideas as suggestions rather than giving orders |
| • Winners and losers, competition, elaborate systems of rules and arguing about them | • Don't challenge each other directly (subtle, behind the scenes if at all) |
| • Low status via being pushed around jockeying for position | • Not accustomed to outward jockeying for position |
| • Keeping track of who gives orders | • More concerned that they be liked |

| | |
|---|---|
| • Boasting about skills and status | • Simply sit and talk |
| • Arguing about who or what is best | • Concerned with harmony and unity |
| • Openly competitive | • Openly cooperative |
| • Concern for status | • Concern for connection |
| • Stress on independence | • Stress on intimacy |
| • Top or bottom (hierarchical) | • Close or far (relational) |
| • Control | • Closeness |
| • Report talk (facts, data) | • Rapport talk (intimacy) |
| • Logic | • Experiential |
| • Literal, Concrete | • Meta-messages |

## REPORT TALK as compared to RAPPORT TALK

Another very important difference between males and females is the reason for which they use verbal communication.

Boys and men engage in *report* talk. Facts. Data. Literal answers to questions. "How are you doing?"

"Fine."

"What happened at school or work today?"

"Nothing much."

"Anything exciting or unusual happen today?"

"Nope."

They talk about "stuff," about achievements, about their work, about sports, about money, about the stock market, and about politics. Very little attention is given to describing how they feel, what emotional state they are in, or indicating anything other than that they have things pretty much in control.

Girls and women, on the other hand, engage in *rapport* talk. Relationships, feelings, people-stuff. They ask questions, not for obtaining literal answers as much as for insight in the feelings of others, for feelings of being included and involved through talking about the answer to their questions. When they get together for conversation it isn't about sports, money, or politics, but about relationships—about families, marriages, children, and who is ill or healthy.

## PLAYING KING OF THE MOUNTAIN
## (OR, THE FRAGILE MALE EGO)

One final difference to understand is another phenomenon we see going on all the time between males and females.

Boys and men are constantly on the lookout for signs of being put down, of being challenged, being told what to do, or otherwise being controlled—because taking what they think to be orders from another person is a sign of low status. A simple question from a girlfriend, sister, mother, or wife, is perceived to be an attempt to play detective or to control. It also can be perceived as an attempt to enter into a secret inner room where he has not decided to let anyone else in. He has a private inner little "clubhouse" where only a secret password gets you in! Little boys are great at building actual secret club houses, whether under the dining room table, with sheets in the bedroom, or hidden places deep in the neighboring woods where only a secret chosen few are permitted to enter.

This is reflected in their relationships as men. This simply doesn't make sense to the girlfriend, sister, mother, or wife. Females interpret the guy's defensive responses to be signs of a lack of love, a lack of commitment, or a lack of closeness.

*For the male, life is a struggle to maintain independence and status.*

Girls and women, on the other hand, are constantly looking for signs of how a relationship is going. Is it getting closer? Is it drifting apart? What are those little inflections of his voice "really" telling me? What was he trying to keep from me when he didn't tell me about going to the store yesterday? When I asked him how much it cost, why did he get so defensive?

*For the female, life is a struggle to maintain relationships and to preserve intimacy.*

Since both of these dynamics are always present in a conversation, it is easy for men and women to focus on different elements in the same conversation. A man and a woman are viewing the same landscape from different vantage points. They are wearing two totally different sets of eyeglasses through which they view life. Words are vehicles through which two almost totally different cultures interact.

Many marriages are in trouble simply because the husband and the wife do not have the first clue about what is going on down deep inside? They simply have no insight at all into the very radical differences between females and males—physically, emotionally, the way the brain functions, how they perceive life generally, or how they use verbal communication to have inner needs met.

## FIXING AND EMPATHY

No one area of difference is more pronounced than how females and males deal with trouble. To the male, trouble means something needs to be fixed. Fix it and the trouble goes away.

For the female, trouble is another opportunity to talk and to share how another feels in the midst of trouble. Fixing the trouble is not as obvious a need to her as is listening to how the other person feels about the situation.

When a man "comes to the rescue" he often misses the boat as far as his wife or girlfriend is concerned. They don't want a "fix!" They want a conversation about the matter. To a male this doesn't make sense at all. Who cares how we feel about the particular trouble being presently experienced? Fix it and everything will be back to normal, the sooner the better!

Thus, he is confounded by his wife's almost angry response to his "solution." "I don't want you to fix it," she exclaims, "I want you to talk with me about it and ask me how I am feeling about it!"

## THE BIG IDEAS OF THIS CHAPTER:

1. Males and females view life from two different perspectives— the male views life vertically and the female views life horizontally.
2. Key elements of the male perspective are top or bottom, independence versus loss of control, status versus loss of status, winning versus losing.

3. Key elements of the female perspective are close or far, intimacy versus isolation, cooperation versus separation, and intimacy versus loneliness.

4. The friction that occurs in every marriage often arises from the differing perspectives by which males and females view life. Marriage is not really a game in which the male plays the game of running away from closeness or intimacy or the woman plays the game of super sleuth and control. What really is at work are two totally different sets of eyeglasses through which they perceive life. One seeks to escape being controlled and the other seeks to prevent the loss of intimacy.

5. Recognizing these gender differences can free two married people from the tendency to over-psychologize their mate's intentions and motives, which happens when they view the other through their own biased glasses. The need is to concentrate on meeting each other's needs. When they understand and yield to these differences, they can learn to compensate for them and learn how to go about things differently for the sake of meeting the needs of the other.

## QUESTIONS FOR FURTHER THOUGHT AND DISCUSSION

1. Does Dr. Tannen's description of how little boys and little girls play seem to be true to your observations and experiences of little children at play?

   - What goes on in a pick-up game of baseball involving boys? Who chooses sides? Who gets to choose team members first? Who gets chosen last? What are the criteria used? Who gets to bat first? What happens when one team supposes that the other team has broken the rules of the game?

   - What goes on in a game of jump rope involving girls? Who chooses sides? Who gets to jump first? Who is left out? Does the involvement focus on the rules of the game?

2. Explain what Dr. Tannen has in mind when she states that the difference between males and females is so profound and basic that two siblings — a boy and a girl — can grow up in the same household, but essentially they will have grown up in two different cultures, in two different worlds of words and perspectives, speaking and hearing two totally different languages.

3. Do you agree or disagree with the following statement? Explain your answer. *"These two vantage points, as two distant mountain peaks, are present in most male/female conversations. It is not a matter of attempting to dominate, on the part of one, or to retreat and hide, on the part of the other, but viewing life through two sets of eyeglasses."*

4. How can adequately recognizing these gender differences free two married people from the tendency to over-psychologize their mate's intentions and motives (which are essentially misread) and to concentrate on meeting each other's true needs?

5. What aspects of their future marriage will tend to be more harmonious and free from strain if two people who are still preparing for marriage understand this information?

6. In what specific ways and in what specific settings could a guy or a girl begin to cultivate a positive sensitivity towards members of the other gender through using the insights gained in this chapter?

7. Create a case study involving a male and a female, highlighting the dynamics that go on in male/female verbal communications. Tell your story in the context of neither party being aware of Dr. Tannen's findings. Retell the story from the perspective of two parties who both are aware and sensitive to the dynamics that go on in male/female verbal communications. (It is assumed that in the second retelling of your case study that both parties are willing to reach out to the other person! It would be interesting to cast your story in a context where one party is sensitive and willing and the other is knowledgeable but not willing to reach out to the other.)

## FOR FURTHER EXPLORATION:

Read: *What Wives Wish Their Husbands Knew About Women*, James Dobson, Wheaton, Ill.: Tyndale House Publishers, Inc., 1975.

Read: *You Just Don't Understand: Women and Men in Conversation,* Deborah Tannen, New York: Ballantine Books, 1991.

Use the Internet: Using one of the many search engines available, explore the numerous web sites and articles that discuss male/female verbal communication differences.

## TESTING YOUR UNDERSTANDING OF FEMALE/MALE COMMUNICATION DIFFERENCES

From your reading of this chapter, see how well you can identify the subtleties of difference between the female and the male perceptions of life and how those perceptions impact verbal communication.

**True or False**

_____ 1.  Much—even most—meaning in conversation does not reside in the words spoken at all, but is filled in by the person listening.

_____ 2.  Friction arises in verbal communication because boys and girls grow up in what essentially are two different cultures.

_____ 3.  Males find themselves in more potential conflicts than females do in growing up because males are always alert to attempts by others to refuse them involvement in intimacy.

_____ 4.  Men tend to make more decisions without consulting their partners, except where big decisions are concerned.

_____ 5.  Women tend to feel it is natural to consult with their partners at every turn when making decisions.

_____ 6.  Men expect decisions to be discussed first and made by consensus.

_____ 7.  The male is always attempting to discover in verbal communication whether the other person is attempting to pull away or to draw closer.

_____ 8.  Girls are not accustomed to jockeying for status in an obvious way; they are more concerned that they be liked.

_____ 9.  Girls tend to not give orders, but to express their preferences as suggestions that are likely to be accepted.

___10.  Gender differences in boys and girls tend not to be displayed until their teenage years.

___11.  Boys tend to monitor what is going on around them and what status they occupy by being on the lookout for signs that they are being put down or told what to do.

___12.  Girls tend to monitor what is going on around them by keeping track of who is giving orders and who is taking them.

___13.  Women tend to try to "fix things," thus driving their husbands, who want simply to be listened to, up the wall and into defensive positions.

___14.  Boys tend to engage in "trouble talk" by concentrating on the troubles of one boy and support him with such statements as, "I know how you feel." Girls tend to shift the focus to their own troubles and dismiss the troubles of others as being insignificant.

___15.  For most women, the language of conversation is primarily a language of rapport, using talk to negotiate status.

___16.  For most men, the language of conversation is primarily a language of report, using talk to negotiate relationship.

___17.  Sadly, but truly, men often view listening as being an underling, and telling as being in charge.

___18.  A woman who expects her listener to be active and enthusiastic in showing interest, attention, and support, will tend to interpret her husband as not really listening at all, but he really is, since men tend to listen in silence with little visible feedback.

___19.  "Let's" is an expression intended by a woman to involve her husband, but to him when she says "Let's," it is felt to be another attempt by her to control him.

___20.  A man who fears losing freedom pulls away at the first sign he interprets as an attempt to "control" him, but pulling away is just the signal that sets off alarms for a woman who fears losing intimacy. Her attempts to get closer will aggravate his fear, and his reaction—pulling further away—will aggravate hers, and so on, in an ever-widening spiral.

Answers to the above: TRUE statements are #1, 2, 4, 5, 8, 9, 11, 17, 18, 19, and 20. FALSE statements are #3, 6, 7, 10, 12, 13, 14, 15, and 16.

#3 is false because being brought closer into a relationship and/or moving more deeply into intimacy are the very things he tends to shy away from.

#6 is false because the male tendency is not to talk much about a matter in the early going, because self-reliance is a major issue in keeping status and control. Only after he is pretty certain how he wants to do something does he talk about it.

#7 is false because the male is virtually immune towards and very insensitive to issues like closeness and intimacy. Status is more important than closeness, and independence more important than intimacy

#10 is false because even in the way they play games as little children, what kinds of games they play, and where they play them, the differences are evident.

#12 is false because the female is not concerned with who is giving orders to whom. She is more focused upon who is related to whom.

#13 is false because women are not into the tendency to fix things as much as they are focused on talking about them and the resultant feelings that develop from them.

#14 is false because just the very opposite is true.

#15 is false because while it is true that women engage primarily in rapport talk, it has nothing to do with status but rather relationships and intimacy. It is the male who has his radar screen searching for status.

#16 is true in that men are engaged primarily in report talk, but the statement is false because men do not use report talk to negotiate relationship. They use it to keep people from getting too personal.

# Chapter 7

# INTIMACY:
# HERS AND HIS

## INTRODUCTION

Every relationship between a male and a female, whether it is a friendship, a dating relationship, or a marriage, is actually, in terms of perception, *two relationships: his and hers.* The relationship is perceived, evaluated, and maintained according to two very different interpretations. This difference stems in part from (1) how the two genders respond to life around them due to brain differences, and (2) how these two ways of perceiving life show up in verbal communication patterns.

## INTIMACY AND GENDER DIFFERENCES

An equally important (and troublesome, if not understood clearly) difference between husbands and wives grows out of their definitions of *intimacy.* The two definitions of intimacy, hers and his, express the expectations each has for intimacy in marriage. The two definitions are so different and constitute a gap so wide that many marriages are never able bridge them.

At the heart of this wide gap are the basic gender differences we have already observed: the gender difference in the brain and how it functions, and the gender difference in the way females and males perceive life and how they express that difference in *verbal communication*.

Let's review some of the female/male differences we covered in the last two chapters.

- Men tend to be *compartmentalized* in the way their brains function. This causes them to be perceived by women as distant, non-relational, and preoccupied.

- Men tend to use words to do *report* talk. Facts. Data. Concrete responses. Yes, no—brief and to the point. In response to a question from his mother, girlfriend, or wife, "How did your day go?" it seems quite normal to the male brain to respond with, "Okay," or "Nothing unusual," or "Fine," or even with a nonverbal shrug of the shoulder.

- Women tend to be *wholistic* in the way their brains function. This causes them to be able to concentrate on and be interested in a variety of items all at the same time.

- Women tend to use words to engage in *rapport* talk. For instance, if a woman asked another *woman*, "How did your day go?" it would probably result in a fairly lengthy interaction between the two, involving talking about other people, relationships, connections, and feelings. They might spend several minutes or more discussing a whole list of related items. But when asking her *husband* how his day went, she only gets in response an "Okay."

  "What do you mean, Okay?" she asks. His perception is that "Okay means, okay!" "Fine means, fine!" and "I did my job. I answered your question."

- This presents a problem. Report talk, although comfortable and normal for the male, does not tend to satisfy the need for rapport talk, which the female finds comfortable and normal. While the former gives the facts, the latter wants to enjoy relationship through the actual verbal interchange. *The female tends to see verbal interchange as a means to gaining greater intimacy.*

*Both males and females desire intimacy.* They just have different views of what it takes to be loved and respected and to be intimate. Each gender has valid, but different, approaches to love and intimacy.

## HOW MEN TEND TO VIEW INTIMACY

### THE CULTURAL IMPRINTS:

From infancy, the predominant message our society sends to males is that real men don't show their emotions. Real men don't cry, they don't admit when they are scared, they don't talk about fears, worries, or feelings of any kind. They are not to express feelings of inadequacy or being overwhelmed. They are allowed to show feelings about anger, fierce competitiveness, and humor, but those are exceptions to the rule. Men are to be *tough, strong,* and *independent.*

If this was not the case, the common argument goes, how could society convince its young men to compete, to achieve, to go to war, and to conquer giants? Thus, many men grow up to pride themselves on being unemotional and logical thinkers.

So it should come as no surprise that men have difficulty identifying emotions in *others,* or in sharing, understanding, and talking about their *own* feelings. To talk about feelings is a sign of *weakness.* Too much of it is a sign of not being truly masculine.

Boys are taught to be strong and to stand alone. Relationships are downplayed and sometimes made fun of. For instance, what happens to a boy who has strong ties to his mother? What if he talks to her about feelings and builds a close relationship with her, and then relates how much involvement he has with her in conversation with his male friends? He is usually labeled a "Mommy's boy." What boy wants that? On the other hand, a girl can be called "Daddy's girl" and the perceptions are quite different. Extend that out into marriage. If a man consistently includes his wife in discussing much of what they share in common, and if he yields to her point of view out of his close, emotional relationship with her, he is often accused of being "henpecked." Wives, on the other hand, who enjoy and talk about their close, intimate relationship with their husbands are viewed as "fortunate" and "ideal" wives.

The big question is, how much of the unique qualities that seem to mark the male's perspective concerning intimacy is culturally imprinted and how much of it is the result of God's unique design. Some would maintain that there are no differences at all between the two genders, that everything is culturally imprinted. However, we have already examined in prior chapters the very unique physiological, brain, and verbal communication differences that are verifiable. Moses, in commenting on the uniqueness of God's design, said, "Male and female created He them." The plural pronoun gives weight to the difference, not the sameness. They were created in God's image, that is their common essence. But within that common essence, God created them to be "them."

## DOING THINGS TOGETHER AND GIVING GIFTS

For many men, simply *doing things together*, such as working in the garden, washing the car together, painting the house together, or going to a movie gives to them a feeling of closeness. "We might not talk a whole lot when we're doing things together, but it felt good to do it together." But for their wives, that is not enough. Talking about it beforehand, talking about it during the activity, and talking about it when it is concluded, gives her a feeling of closeness and intimacy.

*Giving presents* on special occasions, or doing things for one's wife or female friend, is another way males tend to see as an important way of expressing loving intimacy. On occasion, however, a woman longing for emotional intimacy might say within herself, "The gifts are fine. I appreciate them. But I would much rather have *you*."

## HOW WOMEN TEND TO VIEW INTIMACY

From early childhood little girls concentrate on *relationships*. They usually concentrate on relationships with only *several other little girls*. How well life is going is interpreted not by who is out-achieving whom, but *who is related to whom and how closely*. The most common groupings for little girls involve only two or three girls at a time. Whereas boys form groups based upon abilities, skills, power, and status, girls form groups based upon *who likes whom*. Who is related to whom and how closely, and who *likes* whom are frequent topics of interest and conversation.

For females of all ages, intimacy tends to mean *talking* about and otherwise *sharing* feelings and emotions. Females concentrate on how people *feel* and *relate* rather than on the facts and details of a matter. For example, conversations at parties among women concentrate on children, how they feel about situations their children are encountering, and how they feel about their own life situations.

This is the underlying cause for the fact that it is wives who are usually the ones working hard to keep both sets of parents, his and hers, involved in relationship. Wives are the ones who tend to remember birthdays, buy (or plan what to buy) presents for Christmas, send anniversary cards, and invite parents to dinner. For wives, marriage is not an ending of relationships ("For this reason a man will leave his father and mother . . ." is all too often too literally interpreted by many husbands!) but an extension of a whole network of relationships throughout the extended family.

To summarize, talking things over and sharing feelings and ideas about the relationship itself are what bring feelings of *intimacy* for the female, whether as a young girl or a mature woman.


## THE STRUGGLE BETWEEN THE TWO PERCEPTIONS

A common complaint among husbands is that "I want to do things together, but all she wants to do is talk! I get *tired* of talking! She wants me to tell her how I *feel* about it. How am *I* supposed to know how I *feel* about it. I just *do* it, that's all. There's nothing to *feel!*"

A common complaint among wives is that "He never talks to me about things going on in his life. I learn more from what he tells others when we go out with other people than what he shares with me when we are alone together. It is like digging gold out of a mountain of granite! I have to ask, pull, seek, hint, suggest, and still he doesn't catch on. Why is he always trying to hide his feelings from me?"

Let's go back to an earlier part of this chapter where we looked at what happens when a question is asked the husband by his wife, "How did your day go?" She is looking for clues about his *feelings* about what went on. That's more important to her than what actually went on. She is interested in what went on and with whom, because that would give clues about *relationships*. It would also move their relationship closer to the coveted intimacy.

However, the husband has already departed from that box in his brain called "Work." He is glad to be home, can't wait to eat dinner, and he's pretty excited about the game on television tonight. He's not interested in going back there to the box called "Work" again until tomorrow morning. And even if he *did* jump back into that box, he probably couldn't describe his feelings, other than those of anger, frustration, success or achievement. To the average male mind, work is about *goals, jobs, tasks, achievement, evaluation, competition, and compensation*. It's not about relationships or feelings. Thus, he is frustrated and irritated when someone attempts to make him return to something he just left, and pumps him, in addition, for information and descriptions of feelings.

Let's look at this from another side. Husbands feel that they are showing clear signs of commitment to the marriage by doing their *chores* and by being available to do some of the chores with their wives and children. Wives would much rather spend time *talking* together about the little things going on in their lives.

That causes confusion in the husband, especially after a tough day at work. He works hard at forgetting what happened at work. After all, work has nothing to do with being home with his wife and children. But all his wife wants to do is talk about what went on at work. Who did he see? Who did he eat lunch with? What problems did he face? What is coming up tomorrow? When she gets an angry response, "Hey! I don't want to talk about that stuff. I'm home now," she takes it as a sign that he does not want to include her in that part of his life.

She feels closed out, and he feels hemmed in.

## WHOSE PERCEPTION OF INTIMACY IS RIGHT?

Neither gender is "right." Men do not have to become females in order for their wives to enjoy intimacy. Women do not have to become males in order for their husbands to feel comfortable and fulfilled. We have to avoid buying into what some refer to as "gender conceit," wherein one gender has to capitulate to or imitate the other gender. Differences are real and must be acknowledged. However, some degree of accommodation and movement towards each other is both possible and necessary.

> **Note:** One scary thought in all of this is how society's message to boys and men can interfere with their spiritual relationship to God. If feelings and emotions and fears and frustrations are to be kept inside *oneself*, those emotions are often also kept away from *God*.

If men are to be self-sufficient, then faith and trust become difficult. The apostle John asked a very piercing question. "If you cannot love someone you can see, how can you claim to love someone (God) you have never seen?" That same question could be rephrased: "If you cannot learn to be intimate with your wife, whom you can see, how can you claim to be intimate with your heavenly Father whom you cannot see?"

On the other hand, if a relationship always has to have a high level of emotional intimacy, a woman's relationship to God can be weakened. Not all of God's promises, precepts, and principles are loaded with emotion or feeling. Many are cognitively based. God has not moved away or abandoned one of His daughters simply because she cannot *feel* that He is close at the moment.

## FRUSTRATION IN MARRIAGE DUE TO A PERCEIVED LACK OF INTIMACY

How important is all of this to marriage? Is it something we talk about only in books like this one? Are we making the proverbial mountain out of a molehill? After all, generations of men and women have loved, married, raised families, and have grown into old age, seemingly unaware of all of this discussion about female and male differences, and without a book, a videotape, or an Internet download about differences in female and male perceptions of intimacy!

The growing need for marriage counseling in the last several generations has heightened the quest to identify those areas in typical female and male relationships that seem to break down or cause disruption. One of those areas is intimacy. Increasingly, many women are citing lack of intimacy as a major cause for marital dissatisfaction. In his book, *What Wives Wish Their Husbands Knew About Women*, James Dobson cited ten of the most frequently mentioned causes for depression in married women. Virtually all of them could be grouped under the general heading, "lack of intimacy with my husband."

"Go ask a man how many men he's intimate with," says Michael E. McGill, author of *The McGill Report on Male Intimacy* (Holt, Rinehart and Winston, 1984), "and watch him run." He reported in this study that intimacy is a missing ingredient in many marriages, to the great disappointment of the wives surveyed in his study.

I have used this same question ("John, how many men have you been intimate with this past year?") on many boys and men in approaching the topic of how males tend to avoid intimacy. Like McGill, I have found the question to cause alarm, surprise, and even some embarrassment initially. Most boys and men think that I am questioning their sexual orientation! They do not know whether to laugh, hide, or hit me!

McGill undertook a three-year study that surveyed almost 2,000 men and women ranging in age from 18 to 73. It was primarily concerned with relationships men in general have with friends, spouses, parents and children. What he found was that less than 10 percent of men fully and regularly share their feelings with their wives! The resultant impact this absence of intimate sharing has on their wives is that many women sense and know that their husband loves them, but they don't actually *feel* loved. This is because they do not have a deep, significant knowledge of their husband's inner person.

This same aloofness on the part of the majority of men studied carries over into their relationship with their children. As a result, in most families the mother serves as the "emotional link" between fathers and children. She is the "interpreter," the "go-between," the "peacemaker."

Many of the men in McGill's study admitted to not being more open and sharing with their wives and children because they wanted to retain power and mystery. They reported a fear that to share their feelings would make them weak.

McGill states that he undertook the project because he came to realize that there is a basic foundational difference in the way women and men share emotion and define intimacy.

As a result, many wives reported in the study that they know very little about their husband's work, how much money he earns, and what the complete financial picture is of the family. Some even reported signing their joint income tax returns before the husband completed it.

An interesting conclusion in the study indicates that how long a couple was married had no apparent impact on the degree of intimacy experienced by the couple. Younger couples seemed to report the same relative degree of intimacy and/or lack of it as did couples married for many years. Evidently, intimacy is not something that people "ooze" or grow into. Practice doesn't necessarily make perfect in this case. Younger men are no more skilled at intimacy than older men, and vice versa.

McGill discovered also that this lack of intimacy among men extended to virtually every area of their lives. Even among their male friends and co-workers, intimacy was missing. Although they may have fishing, tennis, golf, and running buddies, male conversation focuses on external issues: politics, sports, investments, lawn fertilizers. Very few men reported having anyone in their life with whom they can freely share deep, inner feelings.

If intimacy is, as McGill defines it, simply learning to open up, to be vulnerable enough to share with another person one's fears, hopes, dreams, and inner feelings, then many men do not experience it.

On the other hand, wives surveyed in the study reported a deep hunger and need for intimacy and a closer friendship and relationship with their husbands. Most of the women reported a basic dissatisfaction with this aspect of their marriages. Many of them reported the lack of intimacy with their husbands to be the major deep disappointment in their marriages.

McGill offered several suggestions to couples who may want things to be different than the conditions reported in his study. He urges a couple to *decide* that their marriage will be different. It is a volitional act of mind and will. He urges wives to share with their husbands what it is that they want. Men lack intuitive insight and simply do not understand this deep female longing for closeness. They can learn, however, through being gently coached by their wives and through rewards that are given (praise, words of appreciation) when they are successful at providing the intimacy sought after.

## IN CONCLUSION

To serve his wife well, the mature man has to work hard at breaking the American stereotype of the tough, independent, unemotional male and must learn to share with his wife more than simply his ideas about the government, taxes, the stock market, or the World Series. She has a need to experience him in the deep recesses of his inner man. The biblical perspective is that vulnerability is a masculine strength.

> *"Husbands, in the same way be considerate as you live with your wives, and treat them with [full] respect as the weaker partner and as heirs with you of the gracious gift of life, so that nothing will hinder your prayers. Finally, all of you, live in harmony with one another; be sympathetic, love as brothers, be compassionate and humble" (1 Peter 3:7-8).*

The suffix "-ate" in English, as found in the term "considerate," above, means to be filled with, to belong to, to be characterized by. The godly husband is to be filled with the quality of "considering" his wife in an ongoing, continual basis. It means to focus on her needs for relationship, belonging, and intimacy. Such a man is truly masculine.

## BIG IDEAS OF THIS CHAPTER:

- For a woman, intimacy tends to mean *talking* and *sharing* about *feelings* and *relationships*, and about their marriage relationship in particular.

- For a man, intimacy means *doing* things together, and is expressed through giving gifts on special occasions.

- Men must learn how to become *connected* in their intimacy, contrary to what they have been told by society. Women must learn how to *disconnect* by not interpreting the responses received from their husbands as indicators of marital commitment or intensity of love.

- Men must learn how to meet the needs of their wives in terms of talking about feelings and inner thoughts, and talking about their *marriage relationship* in particular.

- Women must learn how to understand how difficult it is for a man to talk about feelings and relationships, and to patiently assist him to move to that level of intimacy.

- Women can learn to use words that more *specifically express* what they are seeking. If they want to know about a relationship, they need to ask about it, rather than hinting or leaving clues about which most husbands are totally unaware. If they want to know about how a man feels, they need to ask him to name or describe his feelings. A wife can help her husband grow in this area of intimacy.

- Men must become better skilled at listening for and interpreting *the feelings that lie behind the words* that come from their wives in conversation.

- There is a deep, underlying spiritual issue involved. Wives can learn to teach their husbands how to share and become relational, with a view to *greater intimacy* with God. Husbands can learn to teach their wives how to believe and to trust *propositional truths* in Scripture, apart from how she feels at a given moment.

## QUESTIONS FOR FURTHER THOUGHT AND DISCUSSION

1. What is the major difference between men and women when it comes to defining "intimacy?"
2. Which of the two ways of viewing intimacy is superior? Explain your answer.
3. What is "gender conceit?" How does it deny the uniqueness of what God has designed and created?
4. Does our culture still seem to send boys the message that strong men do not talk about, show, or otherwise express their feelings?
5. What are some of the common causes that inhibit intimacy in men? Which ones are real? Which ones are imaginary? Which ones are fostered by our society?
6. What does the ability to share and talk about feelings have to do with a man's relative degree of strength or weakness?
7. How would understanding the male perspective on intimacy assist a woman in experiencing a greater degree of security and satisfaction in her marriage relationship? What constructive steps could she take to improve the level of intimacy she enjoys with her husband? What should she avoid?
8. What constructive steps could be taken by the husband? What will he have to risk?
9. What differences, if any, might you expect Christ to make in this whole business? Be specific. In your own words set forth a case for the positive impact the Christian faith can have on a marriage relationship with regard to intimacy. If you feel that

the Christian faith makes no recognizable difference, state why you feel this way.

10. Read again the story of the fall of our first parents, Adam and Eve, and the consequences of their fall, in Genesis 3 and 4. How do you think sin inhibits intimacy?

11. To what degree and in what ways should Jesus Christ make a difference in the matter of intimacy for a man and woman who both are Christians? See what Peter says about intimacy in marriage in 1 Peter 3:1–7. Read what Paul says in general to all Christians in Ephesians 4, and apply his teaching to the marriage relationship in particular. Then you will be better able to understand his profound exhortation in Ephesians 5:21.

12. Describe three things you have discovered that can make a difference in your future marriage that you will commit yourself to in order to produce a high level of intimacy for yourself and your spouse.

## RESOURCES FOR FURTHER STUDY:

- *The McGill Report on Male Intimacy*, Michael McGill, New York: Holt, Rinehart and Winston, 1984.

- *Keeping It All Inside: Why Men Can't Open Up to Those Who Love Them*, Michael McGill, New York: Holt, Rinehart and Winston, 1985.

- *What Wives Wish Their Husbands Knew About Women*, James Dobson, Wheaton, Illinois: Tyndale House Publishers, Inc., 1975.

# Chapter 8

# LEARNING TO LISTEN

## INTRODUCTION

Has anyone ever taught you how to listen? I mean to really listen? Have you developed specific skills for listening like you have for reading, playing the piano, shooting a basketball, or any activity for which you have a fairly well developed set of skills?

This is an important question to ask. Why? Because if there are two skills needed desperately in marriage, they are the skills of (1) good listening and (2) good confronting.

Because of *original sin*, none of us are by nature good listeners. Some are better at it than others. But all of us, because of the sin of self-centeredness that lies within us, are more interested in having our own ideas and opinions painted out on the billboard of life than to listen to what other people think or feel. That same sin also makes us often angry, hostile, pushy, and irritable when we have something important to say to someone who fails to listen to us in a satisfactory way.

## BAD LISTENERS

Bad *listeners* are all over the place.

Have you ever tried to get your idea across to someone while they were looking over here and then over there, at this person, and at that person, and all the while giving you the direct impression they could care less about what you were saying?

Have you ever talked to someone who constantly butted in and never let you finish one sentence?

Have you ever taken the risk of telling someone else how you felt about something, only to have them respond with, *"That's dumb!"* or *"You shouldn't feel that way!?"*

How did you feel when you encountered those kinds of listeners? Did they make you feel invited, as their guests, to continue with whatever you wanted to say? Probably not.

That is why the two skills of good listening and good confronting are needed desperately in a marriage if it is to be a joyful and fulfilling relationship.

When poor listeners and poor confronters get married, all kinds of bad things take place. There is no healthy communication. They live with each other in anger and frustration.

This is not what God has in mind for marriage. Listen to the apostle Paul's good advice:

> *"Get rid of all bitterness, rage, and anger, brawling and slander, along with every form of malice. Be kind and compassionate to one another, forgiving each other, just as in Christ God forgave you" (Ephesians 4:31, 32).*

The apostle James adds the following:

> *"My dear brothers, take note of this: Everyone should be quick to listen, slow to speak and slow to become angry" (James 1:19).*

The writer of Proverbs warns us of the necessity of listening to others when they are hurting:

*"If a man shuts his ears to the cry of the poor, he too will cry out and not be answered" (Proverbs 21:13).*

This chapter is about learning to be a Servant Listener and a Servant Confronter.

## SERVANT LISTENING AND SERVANT CONFRONTING

Being a Servant Listener involves imagining yourself to be a Radar Screen, on the one hand, and responding to what you hear as a Servant Responder on the other.

The diagram below visualizes a woman confronting her husband, the latter represented by the radar screen on the right. The grids are filters through which the communication has to pass. The filters are composed of gender differences. Other items that occupy space in those filters include personality types, values, patterns imprinted by the family of origin, one's birth order in the family of origin, spiritual dimensions, and patterns of interacting and relating which have already been established in the relationship.

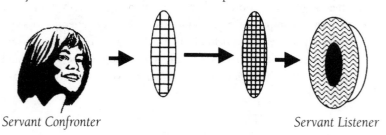

*Servant Confronter*                                    *Servant Listener*

## SKILLS NEEDED TO BE A SERVANT LISTENER

THE FOUR STEPS TO BEING AN EFFECTIVE RADAR SCREEN:

1. **Give to the other person courtesy and honor by <u>inviting</u> them to state whatever it is they want to bring to your attention.**

## 2. Remain _silent_ while they do so.

There is nothing all of us hate more than to try to talk with someone who constantly butts in with his or her opinion, correction, or off-handed remarks.

There is an anatomical law for which I hope one day to be famous. I call it the Wackes Law of anatomy. To test it, do the following. Open your mouth as wide as possible. Try to insert as many fingers as possible into your mouth to widen it to it widest. As you do so, do you feel something happening around your ears? If not, try it again and pay attention to your ears.

The Wackes Law is simply this. When your mouth is open, your ears are shut!

## 3. Identify the _emotions_ and _feelings_ behind the words being spoken.

Words are like freight cars on a freight train. They all look the same, but are very different. The content of each car makes it unique. The same is true with words. They carry meaning. Usually they carry meaning accompanied by emotion. Good listeners attempt to sense the feeling and emotion behind the words by looking at the speaker's face, watching his or her facial expressions, judging the volume and intensity with which they speak, and thereby working hard at the task of listening.

## 4. Give _feedback_.

_Feedback_ is best given by using the exact words spoken by the other person.

Question: _How do you know when it is time to give feedback?_ It is time to give feedback when the other person stops talking . . . and never before! There will be times when, after you begin to give feedback, the speaker will start up again, introducing other statements. What then? Back to step #2—*Silence*. When they stop talking, give feedback again.

Good introductory statements to use when giving feedback are, "Let me see if I got it." Or "Let me see if I heard correctly. What you said was. . . ." And then proceed to feed back to the speaker what you heard.

There are only three responses possible from the speaker after you give feedback:

- "No, that's not what I said at all!"

- "You got some of it."

- "You got it."

If the response you receive is one of the first two, then say something like, "What you want me to hear is really important to me. Try it again. Let me try to understand it again."

If the response you receive is the third response, then move on to the four steps of the Servant Response.

## THE FOUR STEPS OF THE SERVANT RESPONSE

1. No negative statement or retaliation.

   Nothing will kill conversation faster than saying something like, "Boy! That's the *dumbest* thing I have ever heard!" or "You shouldn't *feel* that way," or "Here we *go again*! You're *always* . . ." Another certain conversation killer is, "Oh, yeah! Well, remember the time when you . . . ?"

   No negative statements are allowed! No value judgment statements are allowed! ("That's a *crazy* idea! Where did you come up with that moronic idea?")

2. Give _honor_.

There will come a time later when you can discuss logically and with emotional control the validity or appropriateness of the other person's statements, but not at this point. The major issue is not whether or not you agree with what they say, but rather that you honor them by allowing them to say what they feel, and to listen with careful attention. Honor the person by listening with the intent to accurately hear the words and to ascertain the emotion behind them.

3. Ask the _servant question_.

"What can I do to help?" Or "If you could wave a magic wand over the situation, what would you like to see me being or doing?" Or "What can I do to correct the situation?"

Only a _servant heart_ can ask those kinds of questions. Every cell in our body wants to retaliate, to blame shift, make fun of, or put down. But the servant heart wants the best for the other person, and that includes being listened to, cared for, and assisted to resolve whatever it is that is a problem for them at the moment.

4. Make the _commitment_ to do it.

The servant heart asks the servant question. The servant _will_ or _volition_ makes the commitment to actually do it.

_"Be kind and compassionate to one another, forgiving each other, just as in Christ God forgave you"_ (Ephesians 4:32).

_"Be devoted to one another in brotherly love. Honor one another above yourselves"_ (Romans 12:10).

_"Husbands, in the same way be considerate as you live with your wives, and treat them with respect as the weaker partner and as heirs with you of the gracious gift of life, so that nothing will hinder your prayers"_ (1 Peter 3:7).

_"Submit to one another out of reverence for Christ"_ (Ephesians 5:21).

" . . . *whoever wants to become great among you must be your servant, and whoever wants to be first must be slave of all. For even the Son of Man did not come to be served, but to serve, and to give his life as a ransom for many*" (Mark 10:43-45).

## SKILLS NEEDED TO BE A SERVANT CONFRONTER

### PREPARATION OF YOUR HEART AND MIND BEFOREHAND:

Prepare beforehand. Pray. Get your mind and spirit in line. Think through what you want to say. Write it down if necessary.

- **Own the problem:** "I," not "You" or "We." "There is something that is troubling *me*. I have to talk about it. Do you have a couple of minutes to help me with it?"

- **Don't attack:** attacking presents a new problem. If we begin with a personal attack on the other person, we will never be able to get to the problem that has been troubling us! A personal attack places on the other person's plate something that now has to be dealt with before they are able to help us with our problem!

  A lot of people really get things out of kilter at this point. Their delivery system virtually guarantees that the other person will not be able to listen well. The attack always derails the train!

  "When I approach people about this, I refuse to attack or to put the blame on them. I want them to be able to listen to what I want to say and I want them to be able to feel what I am feeling."

- **Give honor:** you are speaking with God's image bearer. Give honor to God and honor to the other person. Approach people as God receives you. Be gracious as God is gracious.

### STEPS IN SERVANT CONFRONTING

The following five steps to servant confronting must follow the specific order shown to be effective.

- Ask the *Servant Question*:
  *"Something is troubling me. Would you please help me with it?"*
  (*Did you note that there is a servant question for both the one confronting and the one listening?*)

- Name the *Action* or *Activity* that troubles you.
  Be specific. Name it. "When you . . ."

- Name the *Consequences* that have taken place as a result of the action.
  "When you . . . the consequences were, (or) . . . the impact that it had, (or) . . . what happened was . . ."

- Name the *Emotions* or *Feelings* that you now have as a result.
  Be specific and clear. "When you took my (book) to study without asking me, I couldn't study for the test as I had planned. I felt really *frustrated, angry,* and *of little worth* because you didn't ask me first."

- Offer a *Solution* that would be more helpful next time.
  "The next time something like this comes up, I would appreciate it if you would . . ." Or "Something that you could do that would really help me, would be to . . ."

## CONCLUSION:

This might at first seem to be complicated. "Isn't it easier to just argue?" Yes, it certainly is, but it will not be nearly as productive.

Nothing worthwhile is learned without study and practice. Practice the steps with someone you know. The next time a disagreement or argument takes place, try your hand at using the skills of the Servant Confronter. If you sense in another person a problem that you are a part of, try using the skills of the Servant Listener. See what happens!

It will amaze others and catch them off guard! No one expects others to sincerely listen with a servant's spirit! It shocks them when they are not rebutted or counter attacked.

No one anticipates being confronted with humility, kindness, and with honor. They usually have experienced wrath of all kinds, angry words, and personal attacks. They may never have met someone who honors them, owns the problem without placing blame, and who courteously asks them to consider a solution.

The reason you should use the skills of the Servant Confronter in the order they are found above is to help the other person to identify the problem and its consequences. Most of us are very used to beginning a confrontation with statements like, "You make me so angry!" or "I'm so angry with you that I could . . ." That is putting the cart before the horse. State the problem, state the consequences, help the other person see what the impact was on you, and help them to identify with your feelings.

It works much better than the ways we usually employ. Try it. You'll be glad you did!

## BIG IDEAS OF THIS CHAPTER:

1. Servant listening is a skill that is necessary for good communication in marriage and is necessary for the sacred covenant of marriage.
2. Servant listening is a skill anyone can learn.
3. Servant listening gives honor rather than judgment or retaliation.
4. Servant listening tends to encourage and improve intimacy in marriage.
5. Servant listening responds with a servant heart to the well-being of the other person.
6. Servant listening is easier to do when listening to one who is a Servant Confronter.
7. The Servant Confronter approaches the other person with honor, not anger, and owns the problem, rather than blaming the other person.
8. Servant confronting focuses on behavior, consequences, and emotions.

THINGS TO TRY AND TO DO:

1. Sit in groups of two. Sit back to back. One person is the speaker and the other the listener. The speaker tells the listener about a problem they have recently faced. Neither person is allowed to turn his or her head or body. Both have to face straight ahead. Then take turns after the problem has been described.

   How did it feel to have to try to explain your problem to someone who was not looking? Was it frustrating?

2. Try it again with the same person. This time sit face to face. One tells the story, the other listens. The listener, however, gives his or her attention to everything else in the room except the teller. Work hard at appearing to be disinterested and bored. What feelings emerge?

3. Try a third exercise. Use the steps of the Servant Listener and the Servant Confronter. Then change roles. How did it feel? Did it work better than the two approaches tried first? Did it work better that trying to talk to an interrupter? Did it work better than being confronted by an attacker?

# Chapter 9

# ME? A PRIEST?!

## INTRODUCTION

What is a husband? If I dropped onto planet earth from outer space, and asked the meaning of the term "husband," how would you define it? What is a *husband*?

In the marriage ceremony, the minister asks the important question to the bride, "Will you take this man to be your lawfully wedded *husband*?" And at the conclusion of the ceremony he says, "I now declare that you are *husband* and wife." What *is* a husband?

## BACKGROUND OF THE TERM:

The term "husband" comes to us from Old English and is a combination of two words, "hus," plus "bunde." "Hus" was the Old English term for "house" or "household." A "bunde" was a master, or a manager, or the keeper of a vineyard. Webster's Unabridged Dictionary of 1913 defines "husband" as "the male head of a household; a married man."

Thus, we know that according to etymology the term "husband" refers to the manager of a household and, more specifically, refers to a married man who serves as manager or head of a household. *By position, "husband" is the married man who is manager of the house or household.*

But we also have to define "husband" by biblical interpretation, by what the person occupying the position of "hus/bunde" is to do and to be in God's sight and according to God's plan and purpose for marriage.

## ACCORDING TO THE BIBLE:

*In the Bible* the term "husband" is defined as a married man who, in his relationship with his wife, imitates Christ's relationship with the Church. He is the head of his marriage and household, and is the imitator of Christ in his loving and sacrificial care of his wife. The two clearest passages in the Scriptures that define what it means to be a "husband" are Ephesians 5:21-33 and 1 Peter 3:7.

## POSITION AND FUNCTION BIBLICALLY:

In Paul's teaching (Ephesians 5) "husband" is defined both by position and by function. The apostle Paul compares the husband to Christ and to Christ's relationship to the Church. Christ is the model. The husband is patterned after Christ. The husband lives with his wife in imitation of Christ's relationship with the Church.

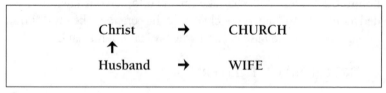

**Chart 1**

Positionally: "The husband is the head of the wife, as Christ is the head of the Church, his body, of which he is the savior" (Ephesians 5:23).

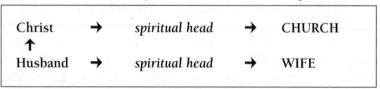

**Chart 2**

## HOW IS CHRIST HEAD OF THE CHURCH?

- He leads the way. (Romans 15:5; John 10:4, 5; Hebrews 12:1, 2)

- He sets the example. (1 Peter 2:21; John 13:15)

- He accepts accountability for us as our representative head. (Hebrews 12:1, 2; 2 Corinthians 5:21)

- He holds final authority. (Matthew 28:18)

*Functionally:* **The husband is to** *imitate* **the** *behavior* **and** *activity* **of Christ.**

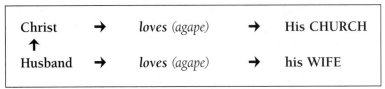

**Chart 3**

## WHAT IS LOVE?

Love (agape) is not a mere feeling or affection that Christ shows and that the husband imitates. Love is an *action verb*—it is something that someone does to or for another person. Divine love, the kind that Christ shows to us, and the kind that the husband is to imitate, is a radical, selfless giving of oneself to meet the deep needs of another. "Christ gave himself up for the church," said Paul.

In Romans 5 Paul defines love again when he says, "But God demonstrates [*shows*] *his own love* for us in this: While we were still sinners, Christ *died* for us." God did not merely talk about loving the church. He did not simply read books about the topic. He did not settle for a correct dictionary definition of the term. No, God *shows* His love for us in that while we were still sinners, Christ *died* for us." Christ *demonstrated* his love for us even to the point of dying for us.

This, then, is the example the husband is to follow. The imitation of Christ centers on a husband's willingness to give up his comforts, his settled surroundings, the idea that he must have his own way, and even his life, for his wife. Jesus said of Himself, ". . . . the Son of Man did not come to be served, but *to serve*, and to give his life as a ransom for many" (Matthew 20:28).

| | | |
|---|---|---|
| Christn→ | *loves=GIVES self up for, died for, meets needs of* | → Church |
| ↑ | | |
| Husband → | *loves=GIVES self up for, died for, meets needs of* | → Wife |

**Chart 4**

Is a man actually called upon to die for his wife? How can a man follow Christ's lead in this matter? Does he throw himself in front of a car or jump off a cliff to show that he loves her? Obviously not. Should he love her to the point of being willing to die for her if necessary? Certainly. There are men who have died physically in the defense of their wives.

But there are other equally important ways of dying. There is a more fundamental dying to his own ideas, goals, and preferences that may be what it takes to fulfill his duty to his wife. There is a dying to the idea of having to have it go his *way* all the time, having to have it follow *his* plan, having to have it done according to *his* timetable, and insisting on *his* wishes and desires. Whatever it takes to assist his wife to grow spiritually, that is what the godly husband is willing to do, in his imitation of Christ.

Sadly, most men, when marrying, think little about or know much about this spiritual side of the marriage relationship. And yet, that is exactly what God has designed marriage to be: a spiritual partnership between a man and a woman. In that partnership the man serves as the loving priest, the spiritual lover.

Paul carries the idea even further. Christ gave Himself up for the Church in order, He says, to *purify* the Church, to make her holy, to cleanse her through the washing of the Word.

The spiritual husband accepts the responsibility and determines to seek purity and holiness in his wife, just as Christ purifies the Church to make her holy, to cleanse her "through the washing of water with the word."

| Christ | → Love's goal: to *purify*: make holy, cleanse → | Church |
|---|---|---|
| ↑ | | |
| Husband → | Love's goal: to *purify*: make holy, cleanse → | Wife |

**Chart 5**

Christ's goal is to present the Church to Himself as a pure woman, without stain, wrinkle, or any other blemish. Likewise, the husband, as priest, strives to do whatever is necessary to be able one day to present his wife to the Lord as a deeply spiritual woman. She might be wrinkled with age at 90, but can be, at the same time, pure and radiant in spirit before the Lord.

Obviously, the husband is not Christ. He cannot purify *himself*, let alone his *wife*. But he can minister to her and be her spiritual encourager and companion.

From among all the other men on planet earth, he was chosen by God to be the instrument in the Lord's hands to encourage Christlikeness in his wife, this special and chosen daughter of the King!

| Christ | → | *Goal: PRESENT her as a pure bride* | → | Church |
|---|---|---|---|---|
| ↑ | | | | |
| Husband | → | *Goal: PRESENT her as a pure bride* | → | Wife |

**Chart 6**

Christ does all this in such a way that the Church can rightfully be called a "radiant" bride or wife. A radiantly pure woman is free from hang-ups, is not bothered by the cares of a pagan, godless culture, knows where she is headed spiritually, and knows Who it is living within her. When she understands all of this and lives in the light of it, she glows, *radiates*, shines! (*Ephesians 5:25, 26*).

| Christ | → | *Goal: a bride who* **RADIATES,** *glows, shines* → | Church |
|---|---|---|---|
| ↑ | | | |
| Husband → | | *Goal: a bride who* **RADIATES,** *glows, shines* → | Wife |

**Chart 7**

Sadly, some women do not shine, glow, or radiate. Can the source of the problem, at times, be traced back to her marriage and to the absence of a husband who serves well as a priest in her life?

The role and position of "husband," therefore, is an intensely spiritual role and position. It is the imitation on earth, within marriage, of Christ and his leadership over, love for, and supreme act of sacrifice for, the Church. The husband is an imitator of Christ in a deeply spiritual relationship with his wife.

## THE PRIEST AND THE EIGHT MARRIAGE PATTERNS

If we go back and review the eight marriage patterns in American culture (see chapter 1), and if we keep in mind the intensely spiritual nature of the role of husband (see above), in which of the following patterns does the husband effectively live out his role as priest?

| | | |
|---|---|---|
| Pursuing/Passive? | Yes___ | No___ |
| Adolescent/Adolescent? | Yes___ | No___ |
| Pursuing/Preoccupied? | Yes___ | No___ |
| Actor/Actress? | Yes___ | No___ |
| Boss/Employee? | Yes___ | No___ |
| Child-Centered? | Yes___ | No___ |
| Doctor/Patient? | Yes___ | No___ |
| Committed/Committed | Yes___ | No___ |

**The godly husband (hus+bunde) is called to be a spiritually and emotionally mature man upon whose shoulders rests the welfare of his wife and his entire household.**

**Several conclusions can be drawn about what being a husband/priest is not:**
1. It is not an easy or casually undertaken role.
2. It is not for the unspiritual man.
3. It is not for the self-centered or preoccupied man.
4. It is not for the biblically uneducated or prayerless man.

**Several conclusions can be drawn about what being a husband/priest is:**

1. It is a highly responsible commitment that is undertaken.
2. It is an intensely spiritual activity and life process.
3. It is for the spiritually mature and firmly committed man.
4. It is something to be understood, something for which the skills needed must be developed beforehand.

## BIG IDEAS OF THIS CHAPTER:

1. The husband is a spiritual man who is intensely involved with spiritual issues, and who serves as priest to his wife.
2. He is aware that he must give an account to God for his wife and his marriage.
3. He is a loving man. His love is an action verb.
4. He is a self-giving man who puts the needs and interests of his wife before his own. Yet, as spiritual leader, he also holds in tension what he and she want with what God requires in the Scriptures. Aware of his own inabilities, he relies upon the Word, prayer, and the Spirit of God within his life.
5. He is an obedient man who obeys and lives by the Scriptures. The washing and cleansing come from the steady reading and talking about the Scriptures.

## QUESTIONS FOR THOUGHT AND DISCUSSION

1. Why is so little time given to prepare men for this important role of being a godly husband?
2. What are some of the better ways to teach and train a boy and young man in preparation for marriage?
3. Why is so little time given to prepare women for marriage to a godly priest?

4. What would be the several best ways to teach and train a girl and young woman to seek marriage to a man who is equipped to serve as a godly priest?

5. What skills would a boy or young man need to develop in order to fulfill the apostle Paul's description of a godly husband?

6. What attitudes or life patterns might get in the way of his functioning in this way?

7. What attitudes or life patterns might prevent a young woman from being ready and willing to receive a man like this into her life?

8 Do you shy away from the term "priest" in describing this aspect of being a husband? If so, what other term would you use instead?

9. Read carefully and prayerfully Ephesians 5:21-33.

## SEVERAL OTHER ACTIVITIES RELATED TO THIS CHAPTER:

### Activity #1

In two brief paragraphs, write for your own reading a description of the following: (1) the uniqueness of the human race from all the rest of God's creation. Read Genesis 1; (2) the distinctive uniqueness of the human male. Read 2 Corinthians 6:14. What does all of this have to do with what is taught in this passage-from a woman's point-of-view and then from a man's point-of-view.

### Activity #2

Answer the following interpretive questions from your reading of Ephesians 5:25-31.

1. What specific action is found in verse 25? What example is given to be followed? To what extent is this action to be carried out, according to verse 25?

2. According to verses 26 and 27, for what purpose did Christ give Himself up for the Church? What do you think this means? Try to describe it in your own words. See 1 Thessalonians 5:23, John 17:19 and 1 John 1:9.

3. What is the instrument mentioned in verse 26 that Christ uses in this regard?

4. To what specific matters mentioned in the previous verses does the phrase, "in this same way," refer?
5. According to verses 26-27, what is one of the primary reasons a man should marry? What is his task? What is the instrument he is to use in this regard? What is his function in the life of his wife?
6. Notice that the ancient words taken from Genesis 2, *"For this reason a man will leave his father and mother and be united to his wife,"* actually are used by Paul in this passage to refer to the matter of intensive, selfless love on the part of a husband for his wife and the task of striving to see that his wife becomes more and more a pure, godly woman. That is quite different from the reasons our society gives for marriage, isn't it?
7. In one summary paragraph state the basic teachings of this passage with regard to the roles and responsibilities of the husband.

**Activity #3**
Answer the following questions:

1. What practical things could a husband do to fulfill his role of priest with regard to the use of the Scriptures in the life of his wife? What misuses of this role should he seek to avoid? What common failures or lapses often keep a man from fulfilling this role effectively?
2. What specific things could a husband do to make prayer his primary source of strength as he seeks to be a faithful priest? What would this look like in his personal life? What would this look like in his daily life with his wife? Why do you suppose many Christian men fail at this point in their marriages?
3. What actions could be taken by a woman who desires this type of relationship with her husband when her spouse is resistant to carrying out his priestly role?
4. What habits of life and personal patterns of discipline are important for a young man to develop in his life prior to marriage that would tend to build in him the qualities characteristic of a priest that are described in this section? Does the pattern of being able to "give oneself up" for another

person suddenly take shape in a man's life five minutes after the wedding ceremony? Why, or why not?

5. What habits of life and personal patterns of discipline should a woman who desires a husband that will faithfully carry out his role as priest look for before she agrees to marry him?

**Activity #4**

Here are some questions for your personal and quiet thought.

1. (For men): Will you pledge yourself with mind and will in true agape fashion to prepare yourself now to be capable and effective as a priest in the life of your future wife? Will you pledge yourself to be a priest when you approach her father, requesting of him his permission and blessing to marry his daughter? Will you assure him that you are determined to fulfill this role as priest in her life?

2. (For men): How will you determine if a woman you love is willing to have you serve in her life as a priest? How will you determine if this is what she wants in marriage? How will you know if she will accept a priest in her life? How effective has her father been in her life as priest?

3. (For women): Will you prepare yourself now to receive a man as priest into your life? Have you yielded yourself to God and told Him that this is what you want in marriage? Have you asked Him to send to you a man who is qualified and able to serve as priest? Will you make this ability one of the primary characteristics you will look for in evaluating a man who desires to marry you?

4. (For women): Are you developing in your life presently the spiritual qualities that will make your husband's task as priest a joy and not a burden?

5. (For women): How will you determine if a man you love is willing to serve as a priest in your life? How will you determine if this is what he wants in marriage? How will you know if he will accept and carry out his role as priest? How effective has he been in your dating relationship as a priest?

# Chapter 10

# THE GARDNER

## INTRODUCTION

We know that Jesus did not marry during his earthly ministry, yet his teachings revolutionized marriage. Did any of the apostles marry? We know for certain that one did, Peter the fisherman. We know that he was married because Jesus healed Peter's mother-in-law early in his ministry (see Mark 1:29-31). Furthermore, according to Eusebius, an early Church historian, Peter was married. When Peter was put to death in Rome by the emperor Nero, according to Eusebius, Peter requested that if he was to be crucified that it be upside down. He made this request with the conviction that he was unworthy of dying in the same manner as did Jesus. Eusebius then states that Peter's wife also was put to death on the same day as her husband, and that the guards required Peter to look on as they led his wife to her execution.

Thus, Peter was well qualified to give clear instructions to Christian husbands concerning their important duty towards their wives (1 Peter 3:7). In this passage, under the guidance of the Holy Spirit, he gives perhaps the most sensitive instructions to husbands in the care and nurture of their wives of any passage in Scripture.

It probably was no picnic for Mrs. Peter to be married to this energetic, mercurial man. She experienced the consequences of Peter's three-year hiatus from his employment in order to follow Jesus of Nazareth. She was there to suffer with him through the agony and aftermath of his denial of Jesus. She was probably with Peter and the others in the locked room when they secluded themselves after Jesus' death. She was probably there with her husband when the resurrected Christ appeared to them in the room where they had gathered, scarcely able to believe what Peter and the several women who had run to the empty tomb told them had occurred. And Mrs. Peter was with her husband at the end, when, at the hands of the emperor, Peter and his wife were put to death because of the Gospel.

The apostle Paul, in Ephesians 5, focuses on the *spiritual* dimensions of marriage and urges the godly husband to serve humbly as a priest in the life of his wife. Peter, on the other hand, in his first general epistle (1 Peter 3), urges the godly husband to be considerate and thoughtful of his wife's needs, respecting her position as the "weaker partner" and as his co-heir of the gift of eternal life. The *emotional* needs of the wife seem to be the focus of Peter's message. Perhaps it was because Peter tended to be a rough and tough fisherman, impetuous and impulsive, that he learned much from Christ about loving his wife and caring for her deep, emotional needs. Out of first hand experience, Peter calls attention to the fact that a woman has special needs that are to be met and nurtured by her husband.

A married woman is a complicated, finely tuned and delicate instrument to whom has been given a godly husband to care for and to meet her needs. She is God's special creation with unique needs. She doesn't think like a man; she doesn't reason like a man, nor does she view life from a man's perspective. A woman is often confusing to her husband. He couldn't figure out his mother when he was a boy, was often confused and irritated by his sister, and now is lost in his attempts to understand his wife!

However, God has given to her a man to be her husband, a man to be God's instrument to help meet her important and deeply held needs of the emotions and spirit. He serves as a gardener in cultivating, feeding, and nurturing her emotional needs.

# A WOMAN'S THREE MOST IMPORTANT EMOTIONAL NEEDS

All of us have emotional needs. Both males and females have similar emotional needs, but there are three that in particular are prominent in the female: her need for *Affection*, *Security*, and *Intimacy*.

## AFFECTION

According to Webster's, *affection* is a "disposition of mind," a "tender attachment." It is a decision, a "disposition of mind" that the husband makes to meet his wife's need for affection. He needs a *disposition of mind* in order to meet his wife's need for *tender attachment*.

It is somewhat like a train. The locomotive leads the way, giving power and energy to the rest of the train. In like fashion, the husband's *disposition of mind* pulls along the rest of the train, the *Tender Attachment*.

| Decision | + | Loving behavior | = | Fulfilled need |

Loving behavior includes two key elements: (1) focused attention and (2) romantic love.

## FOCUSED ATTENTION

A study conducted in Boston by Harvard University discovered that, on average, fathers spend approximately 37 seconds per day in conversation with their young children. This paucity of time spent in communication is not very different in the amount of time that many husbands spend in meaningful conversation with their *wives*.

To shower one's wife with attention demands *time* and focus. The old argument that "quality of time" is superior to "quantity of time" doesn't hold water. It is usually simply an excuse. Women desire and need time alone with their husbands. The *kind* of time that most deeply satisfies a woman's need for affection is *focused time*. It takes concentration, uninterrupted time, and specific effort. Focused time is the kind of time that is directed to her specifically, and with her alone, where only the two are in direct face-to-face and heart-to-heart communication with each other, often without words, just enjoying their time together in an undivided way.

## ROMANTIC LOVE

The second key behavior in meeting her need for affection is romantic love.

A survey of married women experiencing some degree of depression in their marriages, as reported by James Dobson in his book, *What Wives Wish Their Husbands Knew About Women*, found that one of the most frequently listed causes of depression was the *absence of romantic love*. Dobson notes that romantic love, as interpreted from a woman's perspective, does not consist in new cars, material possessions, or elaborate houses. Romantic love is the behavior of being courteous, thoughtful, gentle, spontaneous, warm, and becoming focused on her, and her only.

One married woman who keeps a box of birthday, Christmas, and Valentine's Day cards given to her by her husband demonstrates this. In that collection of cards is found not one card her husband purchased at a store. What has been safe-guarded in the box with very special care are those special creations written and designed by her husband with his own special artwork, poems, and messages. Those, to her, were the most cherished displays of affection. They took time to create, thought to develop, and focused on her as his wife and friend. Those cards struck the match of romantic love in her heart more than anything he could purchase, no matter the cost.

---

**FOCUSED ATTENTION + ROMANTIC LOVE = AFFECTION**

---

## SECURITY

A woman's second essential need that her husband is called to meet is *security*.

The survey in Dobson's book mentioned above revealed that the most consistently mentioned cause of depression in married women is low self-esteem.

Dobson notes that for men, self-esteem is directly related to his work. If he feels productive, appreciated, and satisfied with his work, his self-esteem will be at a healthy level.

For a married woman, however, self-esteem is directly related to the degree to which her husband includes her in his life, the degree to which he shares with her the simple things of life that take place on a daily basis, and the degree to which he shares his dreams and goals with her.

Thus, *a husband who indicates by the level of sharing he gives to his wife that he holds her high in his esteem and counts her as his trusted and intimate friend provides security.*

*Negative jokes* about divorce, the attractiveness of other women, "trading her in" for a younger model, and other such insensitive comments, while perhaps offered in jest, are all potentially harmful to a woman's need for *security*.

There are other threats to security. The losses of employment, work-related transfers, speculative investing of the couple's savings, are also other possible causes of a loss of security. Men must understand what a damaging impact such events can potentially have on their wives.

Equally damaging to her need for security are the angry words, the stubborn attitude that refuses to share, to talk, or to say, "I'm sorry." Comparing her to other women or to standards that he has set for her (e.g., weight, dress, performance) also do great damage to her deep need for security. These all do great damage to her deep need for security.

---

**SHARING + COURTESIES + UP-BUILDING = HEALTHY SECURITY**

---

While it is true that a godly woman is to gain her inner security from God and from her relationship with Him, God has also ordained that she should have a close friend, a lover, a source of encouragement and up-building in the man given to her as her husband.

## AFFECTION, SECURITY, AND THE PATTERNS OF MARRIAGE

Let's look again at some of the patterns of marriage that we noted in earlier chapters. What happens to the deep need for security within a woman who finds herself in one of the following unhealthy patterns?

- Pursuing/Passive

- Pursuing/Preoccupied

- Boss/Employee

- Doctor (Nurse)/Patient

- Actor/Actress

- Adolescent/Adolescent

It is easy to see that in each of these marriage patterns a woman's need for security receives devastating blows, just as if her husband took an ax and began chopping away at the tree of her life.

Sharing with her, and paying consistent attention to courtesies, compliments, and in general building her up in a godly way, are the steps to creating a healthy sense of security in her.

Only the Committed/Committed marriage pattern fully meets a woman's need for affection and security.

**Let's imagine these two needs of Affection and Security as trees growing in a garden.**

*Trees can either be lush and green, or dried up and dead. The amount of sunshine, water, and nourishment they receive, and the quality of soil in which their roots grow make the difference.*

In this sense, the husband acts as a *gardener*. He cares for the needs of his wife just as he would valuable trees in a garden. He watches, inspects, thinks about, and studies to learn more about those needs. He gives time to them. He concentrates on them.

Unfortunately, most men could not even *name* the basic emotional needs of their wives and daughters, let alone pay attention to them and cultivate them.

As a result, many women are discouraged, find little joy in their marriages, and have very few leaves on their emotional trees.

Whenever you find a woman who is bitter, angry, discouraged, strident, or dispirited and lifeless, a place to look for possible causes is her husband and the amount of time and care he is giving her as her gardener.

## INTIMACY

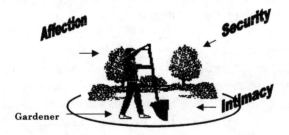

*Intimacy* is the soil in which affection and security grow. It is the third of the female's most important emotional needs.

Picture in your mind a beautiful, well-groomed garden in the cool of the day. Growing in the middle of that garden are two lush, green trees. One tree represents the emotional need of *affection*, the other, *security*. The soil in which they thrive and grow is *intimacy*.

Rich, fertile soil is necessary for lush, verdant trees. Without it, skinny, leafless trees, vulnerable to disease and wind develop. Lush gardens don't just emerge. They are the result of a careful and tire-less gardener.

## PETER'S INSTRUCTIONS (1 PETER 3:7)

It is exactly this that Peter had in mind when he teaches husbands to care for their wives and their needs. Note the specific terms he uses.

- *Be considerate as you live with your wives.* Any word in the English language with the suffix "-ate" means "to be filled with." Hence, the husband is to be *filled with the act of considering* his wife and her needs.

- *Treating her with full respect.* When we respect someone, we honor them, and revere them; we treat them with dignity and full attention.

- *Remembering that she is your spiritual sister, your co-heir of the gracious gift of life.* She is God's daughter. That is her deeper relationship with her husband. It is deeper than marriage, a relationship that is confined to this earthly life. Our relationship to each other in Christ is eternal.

Peter then ends his instruction with this warning. "Be a careful gardener in her life, so that nothing will hinder your prayers."

A clear principle is found here. The man who ignores the needs of his wife or runs roughshod over them is a man who can pray until he is blue in the face; he can be a minister, an evangelist, a foreign missionary, an elder or deacon in the church; but if he is not first and primarily concerning himself with gently caring for the emotional needs of his wife as a gardener, everything else he does is a waste of time and is not acceptable to God.

It is the role of *Gardener* that Peter has in mind when he teaches husbands to care for their wives and their needs.

## WHAT IS INTIMACY?

In the earlier chapter describing the differences between men and women it was noted that the two genders have a very different concept of what intimacy is. It was also noted that intimacy is virtually a missing ingredient to the life and experience of most men. The tough, macho "I can make it on my own!" attitude of the American male works against his ability to become intimate with his wife. While they, too, desperately need intimacy, many men do not recognize the fact.

For the female, intimacy means talking, sharing, being vulnerable. Intimacy, at first glance, means sex for the male. But sex and intimacy often have little in common for the female. The sexual side of marriage only takes on importance and meaning for a woman when it is the product of the sharing of two persons who have first learned to be confiding, sharing, intimate friends. Many married women state that sex in marriage "leaves them cold." What they are saying is that the basic relationship of affection, security and intimacy, which free a woman to give and receive fully in the sexual side of marriage, is missing.

This is why the little things that communicate affection, attention and romantic love have a great bearing for the woman with regard to her ability to respond warmly and sexually to her husband in marriage.

## HOW CAN MEN LEARN INTIMACY?

Women can help their husbands to learn the benefits of intimacy by teaching them how to experience it through creating for them nonthreatening situations where it can naturally occur.

One woman caught her husband by surprise when she announced that she, too, would take up jogging. Her husband had previously taken up the sport to relieve the stress and pressures of his work. She discovered that when the stress and pressures were reduced in his life, he more freely shared himself with her in conversation and activity. She concluded that if she could be with him as the stress and pressures were being released, she could benefit from longed-for intimacy. "When you relax you open up more," she told him one night when jogging together. "It hurts me to run, but it's worth the pain just to have you share with me."

Another woman, whose story was told by James Dobson in his book, *What Wives Wish Their Husbands Knew About Women*, settled, unfortunately, for something far less. One day, in conversation with a friend, she indicated that when her salesman husband finished dinner each night he would make telephone calls to his contacts for the next day. When he talked to them on the phone, she told her friend she would stop doing the dishes to sit and listen to his voice as he spoke with others; so hungry was she for his attention and for intimacy! "He doesn't talk to me very much," she said, "and so I drop everything to listen when he talks on the telephone. It feels good just to hear his voice, even if it is in conversation with someone else on the telephone."

## CONCLUSION

The vibrant, glowing, enthusiastic women in God's kingdom are those women who are fortunate to have for husbands men who have worked hard at developing within themselves those skills necessary to meet the basic emotional needs of their wives. To meet those needs is more important to these men than their jobs, hobbies, recreation, or even their own personal needs. The fruit of their labor are women possessing deep beauty of the soul as described by Peter (1 Peter 3:1-6).

## BIG IDEAS OF THIS CHAPTER:

1. Every woman has three distinct emotional needs—the need for affection, the need for security, and the need for intimacy.

2. Her husband is to act as a gardener in her life, cultivating the two trees of affection and security, and providing nourishment to the soil of intimacy.

3. A woman who is cared for in this fashion shines and glows. Her trees are filled with lush leaves. The woman who is not cared for in this fashion dries up and withers.

4. A husband's spiritual life and effectiveness in prayer is directly impacted by the degree of commitment he gives to fulfilling his role as Gardener.

## QUESTIONS FOR FURTHER THOUGHT AND DISCUSSION

1. Notice the difference between the husband's role as Priest and as Gardener. The first cares for his wife's spiritual needs. The second cares for her emotional needs. Where in his total list of priorities would you think these two tasks should be placed? Are there any priorities that come before these two? If so, which ones? Why?

2. Review the Eight Marriage Patterns covered earlier. Which of those patterns provide a suitable environment for the Gardener to function effectively?

3. Review the Seven Family Types. Which of those types would most likely be headed by an effective Gardener? Why?

4. What dispositions and/or attitudes have to be present in a woman if her husband is to function effectively as a Gardener? Review what Peter says in 1 Peter 3:1-6 about the kind of woman who responds well to an effective Gardener.

5. If a man is ignorant of his role as Gardener or Priest, or if he resists fulfilling these roles, what is Peter's advice, given his teaching in 1 Peter 3:1-6? As a tough, impetuous fisherman, it is not unlikely that his wife assisted him in writing this passage, recalling the lessons that she personally had to learn in her marriage with Simon Peter.

6. What do you think Peter means by the warning that he gives in 1 Peter 3:7? What implications does it have for a husband

who is a minister? An elder? A father of children? A business-man?

7.  Consider the man's role, not simply as Gardener in the life of his wife, but in the life of his daughter(s) also:

a.  Do daughters have essentially the same emotional needs as their mother? Do these emotional needs, which are to be met by the Gardener, occur only after marriage or are females born with these needs? Do sons have emotional needs that must be met? What might some of them be?

b.  Who, in your opinion, is intended by God to be a young girl's gardener prior to her marriage? Her father? Her boyfriend? Her teacher? Her youth pastor?

c.  Do you think there is any connection between the degree to which her father meets a girl's emotional needs and promiscuity? Alcoholism? Drug use? Rebellion? Spiritual coldness? What might it be, if you think so? Why not, if you do not think so?

8.  Read Proverbs 4:1-13. Where is a son to receive his instruction concerning not only life in general, but in the art of being a godly husband and father in particular? At what age, do you think, this instruction should begin? According to this passage, of what value is this kind of wisdom that is to be passed on to a young boy or young man? What is promised?

## A FINAL THOUGHT

If a father does a good job as gardener in the life of his daughter, he is, in fact, preparing her for a life of intimacy with her own future husband. Likewise, she is able to discern the type of man who can meet her needs as a gardener by holding up the example of her father in the forefront. This is why many girls whose fathers have failed at this point often marry men who are equally failures. This is the way sinful and destructive patterns are passed form one generation to another. However, this is also the way a godly man can be certain that healthy patterns are passed from one generation to another by the way he prepares his own daughter for marriage. He is, in fact, preparing the home in which his grandchildren and great-grandchildren will be raised.

There are similar benefits to applying these same principles to a man's sons. As a father prepares his daughter for marriage, either positively or negatively, so he also prepares his son for marriage. His son will either be skilled or unskilled at meeting the emotional needs of his wife and daughters. It all depends on how well he was coached by example and by instruction.

Chapter 11

# SPLITTING THE ADAM[1]

## INTRODUCTION

A woman is never more vulnerable than the moment she commits herself in marriage to the man with whom she promises to become one flesh for *the rest of her life.*

In choosing a college or a college major, she can always change her mind and switch schools or majors. When choosing a career or choosing a specific job offer, she can always change her mind if something better comes along. But as a Christian woman, when she commits herself to a man in marriage, it is for a *lifetime.* Now *that* is becoming *vulnerable!*

Big questions suddenly come to mind. Is he who he says he is? Will he do what he says he will do? Will he act and decide as he claims he will? Will he change? Will he be a godly priest in spiritual areas? Will he be a sensitive, committed gardener of my emotions? How can I tell?

## SPLITTING THE ADAM[1]

The wonder, the dignity, the high value of the woman is set forth from the outset of history. God stated in the first chapter of Genesis that everything He had made was good. One thing alone was yet to be completed, He said, after having created everything that was. One crowning moment was yet to take place. One final event was to transpire. One last creative act was yet to be performed. God said, "It is *not good* for man to be alone."

You remember the story. God parades all the animals in the Garden past Adam. Adam gives each one a name. This was done to fulfill his duty to be manager of all of God's creative work. There was another reason. Adam had to realize that not one of the creatures is suitable for him. They could be pets, yes. But partners? Never. Was this a joke? Did God really think that perhaps an ape, or a salamander, or a three-toed sloth could be a suitable partner for Adam? From what we know about God, this was no trial and error process on His part. He obviously had something else in mind. What was it?

It has been suggested throughout the Church's history that several things took place. First, God was showing to the rest of His creation that, although similar in many respects to Adam—they all have stomachs and eyes and ears and hearts—Adam is different, radically different. He is created in God's image. He is above and is over all of the rest of God's creation. He is God's personal manager or steward who God leaves in charge.

Therefore, true fellowship for God's image bearer cannot be found in a relationship with an animal or an insect or a fish. Secondly, God was impressing upon Adam the high dignity that was his as God's image bearer. No one could satisfy his deepest need for fellowship other than another like himself who would also bear God's image—a woman.

While seemingly trite at first, but deep with meaning, it has often been said recently, in the face of unbiblical ideas about a pos-

---

[1]This wonderfully creative term is borrowed from the Roman Catholic author, Scott Hahn, in his book, *A Father Who Keeps His Promise*, Servant Publications, Ann Arbor, Michigan, 1998, chapter 3.

sible third or fourth sexual orientation, that God gave to Adam, Eve, not Steve. There is no sexual orientation problem here.

> *"So God created man in his own image, in the image of God he created him; male and female he created them"* (Genesis 1:27).

> *"The Lord God said, 'It is not good for the man to be alone. I will make a helper suitable for him.'* . . . *So the Lord God caused the man to fall into a deep sleep; and while he was sleeping, he took one of the man's ribs and closed up the place with flesh. Then the Lord God made a woman from the rib he had taken out of the man, and he brought her to the man"* (Genesis 2:18, 21, 22).

## ADAM WAS SPLIT, NOT CLONED.

We don't know exactly how Adam and Eve were united in marriage. Was there a ceremony in the Garden with their animal friends looking on? Did angels attend? Was God, Himself, the minister? How long did Adam live alone before Eve was created? There is good reason to believe that it was on his second day of living that he woke up from his sleep and was introduced to Eve.

What we do know is that this was a special creative act of God to form both a man and a woman. As many have pointed out, the way in which God created Eve was filled with meaning. She was not formed from a bone in Adam's *foot*, implying that she was to be his doormat. Nor was she taken from a piece of his *skull*, placing her on a lofty pedestal in leadership over him. God did not take a disk from his vertebra, implying that she was to stand or walk behind him. No, she was taken from a rib in his side, close to his heart. She was to stand at his side, to be his equally important partner. *It was a splitting of the Adam, not a cloning of him nor a separate creation of a different sort, forming two distinctly different creatures or species. The two were one from the beginning. God created them that way.*

## ROLES AND RESPONSIBILITIES; NOT EQUALITY OR WORTH

The very story of creation itself tells us that when we talk about the differences between men and women, and when we look at the roles and responsibilities assigned to them in marriage by God, we are talking about equality or worth. Both are equal. Both are bearers of the divine image. Both are partners in managing God's creation. Both are necessary for the other in a relationship marked by equality of worth and dignity.

It is not equality or worth that distinguishes between the two, but roles and responsibilities.

In a football game eleven players take the playing field for each team. There may be twenty or thirty more standing on the sidelines. But only eleven at a time can play from each team. When one team has the ball on offense, each of the eleven has a crucially important role to play. Are they all equals in importance? Certainly! But each one, in their equality, has a different set of tasks to carry out. The linemen block. The ends catch the passes. The backs run with the ball or block for each other. The quarterback throws the ball or hands off to a running back. All are equal in importance and worth. But each is assigned roles and tasks. They don't argue in the huddle about who will throw the pass. They don't all break from the huddle and try to snap the ball to the quarterback. Each one knows exactly their role and responsibility.

**It is not a matter of equality or worth,
but of roles and responsibilities.**

## ROLES AND RESPONSIBILITIES OF THE GODLY WIFE

To Eve and to all of her daughters has been given certain roles and responsibilities to carry out in marriage, just as to Adam and all of his sons has been given the roles to be priests and gardeners. Eve and her daughters have their roles and responsibilities. What are Eve and her daughters called by God to be and to do?

### THE HELPMEET

"Helpmeet." That term sounds strangely archaic. "Helpmeet." Does it mean being a helper? Is there a deeper meaning? Yes, there is. The term in Hebrew carries the sense of, "One who brings another to completion or maturity."

## 1. A helpmeet spiritually:

God chooses to use in the life of every married man a wife who is God's instrument to bring him to completion and maturity. He is not perfect. He is not completely Christlike. He is not fully mature spiritually. He is not competent for every task or capable in every situation. Through a wife's prayers, encouragement, conversation, and other interactions, God matures her husband and increasingly forms Christ in him. She is an instrument in God's hands. She is her husband's helpmeet. It is a spiritual responsibility that she has to be used by God to assist her husband to grow and mature into the likeness of Christ.

> **Truth:** *Among all the available women alive on the earth, God has selected her to be His instrument to form and perfect Christlikeness in this particular man, her husband.*

Eve was an instrument in Adam's life for disobedience when tempted in the Garden (*Genesis 3:6; 2 Corinthians 11:3; 1 Timothy 2:14*). (The Genesis account indicates that Adam was standing right there, doing nothing, perhaps "out of it" at the moment, or consenting to what was taking place, at the moment when Eve was confronted by Satan and she yielded to him.)

Through her own spiritual rebirth and growth, the new Eve is intended to be used by God for the spiritual restoration and growth of her husband. She is his spiritual covenant partner (*Malachi 2:14*).

Through patience and prayer she is intended to assist him, to instruct him, to live an exemplary life in front of him so that he will grow into Christlikeness (*1 Peter 3:1-6*).

## 2. A helpmeet emotionally:

Do you remember the three major emotional needs of the woman covered in an earlier chapter—the need for Affection, Security, and Intimacy? The man also has three needs that stand out—the need for Affirmation, Support, and Intimacy.

God has given to the frail male ego, damaged and bent by original sin, a helpmeet to affirm him, to support him, and to encourage him. Through his wife God desires to bring healing and maturity to the man's emotional life.

A Helpmeet is one who fills in the gaps; one who brings another to completion or maturity.

### 3. A helpmeet in God's Service

Since the marriage belongs to God, and since it is acknowledged that it is God who has brought them together, their marriage belongs not to the two but to God. He formed it. He owns it.

Where will they live? Where will they go? What will they do? Those are all issues God decides as he includes the two in his eternal plan. They serve God together for the entirety of their earthly marriage. The godly wife is a partner with her husband in God's service.

For this to take place, the wife has to take seriously her own spiritual life. Her relationship to God through Christ, her knowledge of the Scriptures, the discipline of prayer and meditation that she develops, her degree of obedience to God's Word and God's way are absolutely essential. A spiritual man is hobbled and crippled when he is in partnership with a spiritually weak and spiritually undisciplined wife. Many men have been held back at this very point. They did not have a spiritually mature helpmeet or partner in God's service.

A good helpmeet cultivates her own knowledge of the Scriptures, the disciplines of prayer and meditation, and obedience to God's Word and God's way. If she is to care for him and to be used to nurture him in God's way, she has to be knowledgeable of the Word of God.

Thus, a woman cannot serve as a helpmeet to her husband in areas that she is not willing to go herself, or to cultivate skills and habits that she is not seeking to acquire herself.

### 4. A helpmeet who is his best friend and intimate lover

One serious consequence of Adam's fall was to plunge himself and all of his descendants not only into alienation and estrangement from God, but also from each other. This is especially acute in males. Most men have few good friends. As we saw in an earlier chapter most men have little knowledge about or experience with true intimacy. They are like lost little puppy dogs locked up inside a big man's body.

God's desire for each man is an increasing intimacy with God. However, that often is first experienced through his learned intimacy with his wife. If he cannot be an intimate friend of his wife, whom he can see, touch, and hear, how can he be intimate with a God he cannot see, touch, and hear? (*See 1 John 4:20*) God did not design a snail, eagle, or box turtle to lead a man by the hand into greater intimacy. God gave to the man his wife to be his encouraging guide. Her goal is not only through intimacy and friendship to meet her own needs but, through this lifelong process of marriage, to lead her husband into ever increasing intimacy with her so he can also experience the same intimacy with God, through faith in Christ (*see 1 Peter 3:1-6*).

Paul states it clearly. He exhorts the older women, who have learned this great lesson and who have seen it at work in their relationships with their own husbands "to be reverent in the way they live, not to be slanderers or addicted to much wine, but to teach what is good. Then they can train the younger women to love their husbands and children, to be self-controlled and pure, to be busy at home, to be kind, and to be subject to their husbands so that no one will malign the word of God" (*Titus 2:3-5*).

## YIELDING TO GOD'S PLAN FOR LEADERSHIP, ORDERLINESS, AND ACCOUNTABILITY

To prevent chaos and disorder in the marriage, God assigns leadership to one of the two. To that one is given the responsibility of being the head, the leader, the representative delegate before God. One must give an answer to God for the marriage. One is to serve as leader and head.

The leader and head is chosen for reasons known only to God.

It is not because the one partner is better equipped, more intelligent, better informed, or more valuable. It is not even that one is better at it than the other. But for a reason known only to God, He has given to the husband the role of leader and head.

To this divine plan for orderliness and accountability and to avoid chaos and irresponsibility, the wife is called by God to yield herself to the leadership God has assigned to her husband.

> *"Wives, submit to your husbands as to the Lord. For the husband is the head of the wife as Christ is the head of the church, his body, of which he is the Savior"* (Ephesians 5:22, 23).

She submits not to a more competent, more valuable, more highly skilled husband, but she submits to him as the one to whom the Lord has given the responsibility and the accountability. She looks beyond her husband to the Lord. *She submits to God's way and God's plan, trusting God for the results*, and not to the abilities or skills of her husband.

Knowing that her husband will one day stand before God to give an account for his household and his marriage, the godly wife affirms, supports, and encourages her husband. She wants him to win!

## A REBELLIOUS CULTURE MOCKS THE GODLY WOMAN

Many in our culture misunderstand the orderliness in the family God has designed. They imagine that the Bible teaches the superiority of males. They view the roles and responsibilities assigned by God as confining and enslaving—not only for the wife in her submitting to God's orderliness, but enslaving also for the husband in his required accountability. Our culture praises neither submission to authority nor accountability to anyone higher than ourselves. The demand for one's own way (as sheep who go astray!) flies in the teeth of God's call upon both the wife and her husband. The autonomous heroine and hero in our culture neither yield to others, nor do they accept responsibility or accountability.

As is true with all of God's truth, mankind makes every attempt to question, twist and oppose the truth in Scripture that God has designed to define and guide the roles and responsibilities of the wife and the mother.

All of the roles defined in the Bible for the various family members (fathers, mothers, children) are under heavy attack in our society. Generally speaking, wives and mothers are being exhorted to seek "freedom" from the roles and responsibilities given in the Bible. "Children's rights" are being championed to the point that in Sweden, for example, the law forbids parents to spank their children. Swedish students are told in school that if their parents fail to abide by that law, the children should tell their teacher, who will then notify the officials. Husbands and fathers are made to feel like "dictatorial monsters" if they practice the roles and responsibilities as described in Scripture.

---

A BIBLICAL PRINCIPLE

*No matter what the surrounding society or culture believes and practices, God has promised His blessing to those who remain obedient to His word. Obedience results in God's blessing. Disobedience results in the absence of God's blessing. When His blessing is lost, all kinds of sinful dynamics begin to show up in the family—chaos, selfishness, bitterness, strife, etc.*

---

The supposed glorious liberation of the woman away from biblical concepts of marital roles and responsibilities, and the glorious liberation of the highly touted "free man" away from biblical concepts of responsibility and priesthood, produces slavery, not freedom. It creates a new bondage to self that ensnares and deadens, all the while dressed up in the costume of "Liberation" and "Modernity." It does not liberate. Liberation only comes through obedience to God's Word and God's way.

Jesus summarized it best. "You will know the truth, and the truth will set you free" (*John 8:32*). The autonomous self is the prideful self that does not know God, nor is at peace with God; it is hostile to God (See Romans 1:18). It also becomes hostile in marriage, for where there is no obedience to God's Word and God's way there is no blessing. Marriage without blessing is hostility.

## THE POLITICALLY INCORRECT "S" WORD

While primarily addressing leaders in the church, the principle found in Hebrews 13:17 applies to Christians in all walks of life and in all relationships. It is applicable to husbands, wives, and children. It is the principle of accountability and yielding to the one accountable.

> *"Obey your leaders and submit to their authority. They keep watch over you as men who must give an account. Obey them so that their work will be a joy, not a burden, for that would be of no advantage to you"* (Hebrews 13:17).

> *"Submit to one another out of reverence for Christ. Wives, submit to your husbands as to the Lord"* (Ephesians 5:21-22).

Submission is a duty of all Christians. Bending the knee and the neck before the Lord, and thereby acknowledging that He possesses all authority in heaven and earth (Matthew 28:18-20), enables one to yield to His authority wherever it is found. Christians submit to governments, whether national or local. They yield to leaders in Christ's Church. Husbands and fathers are viewed as those entrusted with God's authority to lead their marriages and families. It is not a burden, but a blessing. It is not slavery. It is a willing yielding from the heart "out of reverence for Christ."

Wives submit to husbands in God's plan for things. Children submit to parents. Employees submit to employers. Citizens submit to godly rulers. Submission is a love expressed through putting the needs and interests of another person in the forefront of one's priorities and effort.

Submission is not inequality or inferiority in terms of value or worth. To submit to God's authority, no matter where it is found, is not demeaning or belittling.

> *"You are all sons of God through faith in Christ Jesus, for all of you who were baptized into Christ have clothed yourselves with Christ. There is neither Jew nor Greek, slave nor free, male nor female, for you are all one in Christ Jesus"* (Galatians 3:26-28).

Submission is not the stifling of talents, gifts, abilities, or insights. Those who yield to God's authority, no matter where it is contained, do not park their brain at the curb or cease to be a creative, imaginative, or productive people. Simply through submission to God's authority, God's image bearer carries out her or his true calling. It is the life of obedience rather than that of sinful disobedience.

While the husband is given the responsibility to manage the affairs of the entire family as its head (*I Timothy 3:4*), the wife is encouraged to be his creative, active and productive partner (*Proverbs 31*). She is called her husband's "helper," his "complement," his "counterpart" (*Genesis 2:18*).

Submission to the authority God expresses through her husband is uniquely the role given to the wife by her perfect, all-knowing, wise heavenly Father. It is an attitude of the heart, not a forced response to an external restraint or control (*I Peter 3:1-6*).

It is a yielding to God, recognizing Him as standing behind and working through the authority He has established (*Romans 13:1-2*).

It is a voluntary act of the will, an obedient assuming of one's God-given role (*Ephesians 5:21-22*).

Submission is a positive, spiritual attitude, a God-given role that fits into God's perfect plan for marriage and results in God's blessing (*I Peter 3*). It is recognition of, and a yielding to, God's order for things. (See Paul's illustration in *I Corinthians 12:12-26*. Although he is speaking there about the various gifts and offices in the Church, the illustration describes the similar situation in the marriage and the family.)

*A motive for the godly woman's yielding to the authority of Christ, as contained in her husband's role as leader, is her devotion to Christ.*

The above statements describing what the Bible means by the term submission clearly demonstrate that it is a matter of the obedient and willing heart to the clear teaching of Scripture and not a grudging, demeaning slavery to a male tyrant.

A spiritually submissive wife always has her eyes ultimately upon the Lord and not her husband. The reason for submission is ultimately her desire to be obedient to the Lord. She sees standing behind her husband the Lord who has given to her husband the role of leadership for her sake and the sake of the marriage. This is clearly the teaching of Paul in Colossians 3:18.

Her obedience to God's desire at this point is rewarded not primarily by her husband but by the Lord. Her individual relationship to God is not damaged by her submission to her husband, but is, in fact, heightened and made more pronounced.

The Lord owns all authority (*Matthew 28:18*). He bestows a portion of that authority to governments for the good of the people, and we all are to submit to those governments as an act of obedience to the Lord (*Romans 13:1-5*). He has bestowed a portion of that authority to the Church, and we are to submit to the elders and the Church as an act of obedience to the Lord (*Hebrews 13:17; I Peter 5:5; Matthew 18:15-20*).

In the same manner the Lord has bestowed a portion of that authority to husbands for the good of the family (*Ephesians 5:23*). Wives are to submit to that authority, for it comes from God (*Colossians 3:18*).

This is especially important when we look at the illustration and example used by Paul in Ephesians 5:22-33. The husband is to love just as Christ loved the Church. The problem is that no husband on earth has ever been able to even closely follow that consistently. No husband is a perfect leader with the wisdom and purity of Christ.

However, the command to be submissive to one's husband does not depend upon his worthiness to be submitted to, any more than the command for the husband to love his wife depends upon her degree of loveliness.

They both do so out of their reverence for the Lord (*Ephesians 5:21*).

## ALL THINGS WORK FOR THE GOOD . . ."

The Apostle Paul teaches that "in all things God works for the good" of the Christian woman (*Romans 8:28*). He certainly would include that human instrument that God has placed in her life, her husband. Likewise, no girl received her father as a result of luck or chance. He is a gift from God "for the good." Paul defines in Romans 8:29 what that "good" is. It is "to be conformed to the likeness of His Son."

Submission is to accept this goal God has established for her, and to accept this instrument God has chosen for her. It is to open oneself to the cleansing, the purifying, and the maturing that comes through living with this man. Hopefully, she will have sought a godly man who is skilled in the Scriptures and disciplined in prayer. Perhaps he will be one who at times wavers. With her eyes focused beyond the instrument, however, to her heavenly Father who does the perfecting, she yields in patience and persistence to the spiritual leadership of her husband (or father) for God's will to be accomplished in her life.

This does not negate the clear word spoken by God prohibiting a Christian woman from marrying a non-believing man (*I Cor. 7:14-16*), as though marriage to a non-Christian will, by the resultant conflict and hardship; produce greater levels of endurance and spiritual grace! Paul has in mind, quite to the contrary, the spiritual relationship a godly woman has with her godly husband through intimacy, the Scriptures, prayer, and a lifetime of experiences together. As Christ's goal is a "radiant" Church (*Ephesians 5:27*), so a woman glows radiantly through such a marriage.

## SEVERAL CONCLUSIONS ABOUT WHAT IT MEANS TO BE A GODLY HELPMEET IN A GODLY MARRIAGE:

- She is a spiritual woman who is intensely involved with spiritual issues.

- She serves God as a helpmeet to her husband, as an instrument in God's hands to perfect and mature her husband in Christlikeness.

- She fulfills a partnership with her husband, as together they use and cultivate their marriage for the service of God.

- She affirms, supports, and encourages her husband in his leadership, because she is aware that he must give an account to God for their marriage and household.

- She yields to the principle of leadership, orderliness, and accountability that God assigns, as unto the Lord.

- She is an instrument in God's hands to meet her husband's need for *Affirmation, Support, and Intimacy*.

## BIG IDEAS OF THIS CHAPTER:

1. The godly wife is a spiritual woman who is intensely involved with spiritual issues.
2. The godly wife serves God as a helpmeet to her husband, an instrument in God's hands to perfect and mature her husband in Christlikeness.
3. The godly wife is a partner with her husband, as together they use and cultivate their marriage for the service of God.
4. The godly wife meets his emotional needs for affirmation, support, and intimacy.
5. The godly wife yields to the principle of biblical authority as unto the Lord, as it defines leadership, orderliness, and accountability for her marriage and household.
6. The godly wife is not bewildered, confused, or discouraged by a surrounding rebellious culture that mocks God's Word and God's way. She only gains true dignity and worth as she follows God's plan for her life, including His leading her into marriage.

## QUESTIONS FOR FURTHER THOUGHT AND DISCUSSION

1. Read several times Peter's instructions for wives in I Peter 3:1-6. Read also his words in 2:13-25.

   a) What is the wife's relationship to be with her husband, as described by Peter?
      i) From the context of 2:13-25, what is the outstanding example that the wife is to seek to imitate as she lives with her husband in obedience to this passage? There are two situations described by Peter in which this re-

sponsibility may have to be carried out. One describes a woman married to a non-believer (3:1-2) and the other a woman married to a believer (3:7). In either case, what are the implications of the words, "Wives, in the same way..."?

b) Define in your own words the beauty that is described in this passage. Compare the beauty you described with what our society says about what constitutes beauty.

c) What do the words, "do not give way to fear," relate to in this discussion (verse 6)?

2. The early Christians had a high and special regard for Abraham. (We should too! See Romans 4.) It was natural for them to be open to instruction about his marriage and family life also. What do you think verse 6 really means? What is meant by "master?" What is not meant? What is the highest prize or benefit described in these verses for the woman who fulfills these precepts?

3. Read several times Paul's instructions for marriage in Ephesians 5:21-33.

a) What does he state in common with Peter to describe the relational role of the Christian wife in her marriage? To whom does 5:21 apply?

4. What example is given as the example she is to follow in this? To what extent is she to do this?

5. What is the primary motivation given in this passage for her to keep in mind as she lives this way with her husband?

6. How would you respond to someone who said, "The problem with what Paul says in Ephesians 5 about the relationship between a woman and her husband is two-fold: (1) the Church submits to a perfect Christ, whereas wives are exhorted to yield leadership to an imperfect husband; and, (2) these are words for an earlier culture, not our culture?"

7. How would you respond to someone who said, "The view of the woman in the Bible consigns her to a life of serfdom, slavery, and of little self-worth"? She is the plaything of her husband. She is merely his housemaid."

8. In what ways could a girl be a "burden" to her father, about which she is warned in Hebrews 13:17? What negative effect could such an attitude and behavior have on him and to their relationship? How would it impact his ability to help meet her needs for affection and security?

9. Respond to the same questions (#8 above) as they relate to a wife in relation to her husband.

10. What new insights as to the dangers of a man reneging on his God-given responsibility for spiritual leadership has this discussion brought to light? What far-reaching implications are involved?

11. Describe the godly woman's role in marriage by responding to the following:

   a. What is the motivation for a woman's obedience to the roles God has given her in marriage?

   b. How can a godly woman support her husband emotionally?

   c. How can a godly wife support her husband spiritually?

   d. Describe the blessing of God that comes to a woman who lives in her marriage God's way?

## AN ADDITIONAL SCRIPTURE PASSAGE TO INVESTIGATE:

Read Proverbs 31 and respond to the following:

1. Does this passage support or refute the teaching that the married woman's only place is in the home? Support your answer with evidences found in the chapter.

2. Does this passage support or refute the idea that men alone are to be income producers? What is taught about a family business as a form of spiritual partnership? Support your answer with evidences.

3. Describe in your own words the godly woman as described in Proverbs 31.

# Chapter 12

# THE MARRIAGE COVENANT

## INTRODUCTION

Marriage is the deepest and most profound of all human relationships. There is simply no other relationship like it in all of life. In marriage a man and a woman bind themselves together by covenant for life. On the basis of the *covenant* vow they take, a man and woman become one flesh (Genesis 2:24; Malachi 2:14; Matthew 19:4-6).

Covenant is not a commonly used term in our culture. It is often confused with the term contract. The two are not the same. We are acquainted with a piece of paper called the marriage *license*. People assume that the marriage *license* is the item that binds the marriage together.

The marriage license is a legal document authorized by the state in which the wedding takes place. It costs a fee to obtain, it has certain requirements that must be fulfilled in order to obtain it, and only certain individuals are authorized to sign the license in order to make it legitimate and binding. The marriage license is a form of contract, but it is not a covenant.

In a wedding ceremony I often hold up the actual marriage license of the couple being married and a copy of the New Testament.

I do this to illustrate the difference between the two forms of agreement—the contract and the covenant. I state that while both the contract and the covenant are present in the ceremony, it is the covenant, not the contract or license, that holds the marriage together and makes it a distinctly Christian relationship.

Contracts and covenants are both a mutual agreement of two or more persons or parties. There are terms and conditions, but there the similarity ends.

Marriage, in the biblical sense, is a *covenant*, not merely a *contract* legitimized by a *license*. A *covenant* is an agreement that binds two people together by *sacred oath* taken in the presence of God.

## TWO MAJOR DIFFERENCES BETWEEN THE CONTRACT AND THE COVENANT.

### 1. PROMISE VERSUS SACRED VOW:

A contract requires a *promise*, made either in writing or verbally. The covenant goes far deeper and involves a *solemn vow*. The promise is sealed with a signature or verbal pledge or handshake. These bind one's name, reputation, and honor: "I promise!" or "I pledge you my word." The *sacred vow*, on the other hand, invokes the name, the presence, and the honor of God. If the *contract* is broken, you have to face whatever the consequences are legally and personally. If the *covenant* sealed with a *solemn vow* is broken, however, you have to give account to *God*, because *His* name was invoked.

There are examples in our culture where both are used together, recognizing the difference between the two and the uniqueness of both. (1) In the American court of law, both are employed. When witnesses are called to testify, they raise their right hands in promise, they place their left hands on a copy of the Bible in oath taking and then state, "I promise to tell the truth, the whole truth, and nothing but the truth, so help me God." "I promise . . . . so help me God." (2) When elected officials are sworn into office, they place their left hand on the Bible, and they raise their right hand as they respond by vow or oath to the questions addressed to them during the ceremony. Evidently our society learned long ago that mere promises and contracts are not sufficient to bind a person to his or her commitment. It probably also means that everyone else looking on feels better if a sacred oath is taken before God.

The covenant is a deeper, more profound commitment. It is made in the presence of God as witness. To break the covenant is to break a vow taken before God. An oath brings the maker under the eyes, authority, and judgment of God.

A contract requires a *promise*, made either in writing or verbally. The covenant goes far deeper and involves a *solemn oath* or vow. The *promise* is sealed with your signature or other pledge and involves your personal reputation if kept or broken. The *marriage covenant*, on the other hand, is centered on the *sacred oath*. The *oath* or *vow* invokes the name, the presence, and the honor of God.

## 2. EARTHLY AUTHORITY VERSUS HEAVENLY AUTHORITY:

The *marriage license* is issued by the state. There are few laws to regulate it. In most states no reasons must be given to end the agreement. Earthly authorities determine the consequences of the termination. If the *marriage covenant* is broken, however, an account must be given to God, because His name was invoked. The *marriage covenant* is the handing over of yourself to another for a lifetime, and constitutes an agreement to live by the principles given by God in Scripture. The *sacred vow* brings the vow maker under the eyes, authority, and judgment of God. The *marriage covenant* goes beyond what is required by law through its marriage license. Courts and laws can say what they will, but the covenant is holy and sacred and under God's authority.

## THE MARRIAGE COVENANT BRINGS ASSURANCE

The marriage covenant assures the wife that even when she is old, wrinkled, gray, and hobbled by arthritis, her husband will be her priest and gardener. He is bound to her lovingly by covenant. If she contracts a horrible illness or disease, he will remain by her side as her friend and partner. He has bound himself to her by oath. He is accountable by oath, not primarily to her but to God. Likewise, the husband has the assurance that even when his weight shifts to his middle, when he gets bald, can no longer run, play ball, or cut the grass due to old age and senility, his wife will be his lover and friend. Should he fall gravely ill or become immobile, she will be there to care for him as friend and partner. She gave herself to him by oath in the presence of God.

In our culture thousands of marriages fall by the wayside. High percentages never last past the fifth anniversary. Others fall apart by the thousands after the youngest child leaves home. Thousands more are miserable, unhappy, and remain in marriage only for its convenience. These people do not understand the concept of covenant and usually are not in relationship to the One in whose presence a covenant is undertaken by solemn oath.

The marriage license is an easily broken contract for many. It is an easily broken contract by law. No one is legally bound to a lifetime of marriage. There are no laws that require it. There are no courts that require a person to maintain the promises sealed by the license. There are no assurances from the contract called the marriage license. The marriage license and a mere ceremony bring little assurance to the ones being married!

The marriage covenant, on the other hand, is a solemn thing. It invites God into the marriage. It invokes Him as the witness to the oaths taken. Because He is present, there is great comfort and assurance about the permanence and future of the marriage. Two people give themselves personally and deeply to each other and to God.

## THE COVENANT IDEA IS CENTRAL IN THE MARRIAGE CEREMONY

In Christian marriage whole families are involved in the oaths of the marriage covenant. The groom vows to the bride's father and family his lifetime gift of himself to their daughter, sister, or granddaughter.

The bride vows to her family and to the family of her husband her lifetime gift of herself to their son, brother, and grandson.

Early Christians understood this fully. In our present marriage ceremonies elements remain from those former days of understanding.

*The bride is given in marriage by her father.* Why do we do this? In some marriages that I have performed, the bride's father has asked, "I don't have to stand there very long, do I?" That confounds me and indicates that he has not a clue about the deep meaning of his presence there with his daughter in the ceremony.

The father took a sacred vow concerning her when she was an infant. Now he responds to the groom's vow to do the same by yielding his responsibility as priest and gardener to the groom. He stands between the bride and the groom until the time in the ceremony when he gives his daughter in marriage. It is an element remaining from a day when everyone understood that the bride was born into her father's household, had been raised under his leadership, that he had served as her priest and gardener up to the wedding day and now was ready to transfer that responsibility over to the groom. As the father took his sacred vow concerning her when she was an infant, now the father is responding to the groom's oath to do the same from this day until her death.

*Parents are seated in the front row.* Why? So they can see better? No. It is a remnant from those days of understanding that the sacred vows, the solemn oaths of the marriage covenant, were being taken in the presence of the two family households from which the bride and the groom had come. It is the acknowledgment that the two families are there, bringing their children to this time of establishing a new marriage covenant, where a new household of faith, sealed by oaths of covenant, is being established.

*The groom enters the sanctuary of the church first.* At the very end of the processional, the bride enters last on the arm of her father. Why the bride last? Why not the groom last? Have you ever seen the groom come in last to the fanfare of the organ? Why not? Why does he not enter on the arm of his mother?

It was understood that the groom had initiated a new covenant. He had invited a woman to enter into marriage with him, to seal that marriage by a solemn oath, by a sacred vow. As the initiator and leader of the marriage covenant, he enters first and waits for his bride to enter on the arm of her father.

*Vows are taken.* Why vows? Are they not merely formalities? Someone once remarked to me after a marriage ceremony that it was probably not a good idea to have two young people make such all-encompassing vows for a lifetime. People lived longer now, she said, and perhaps no one could keep such vows for so long.

The wedding vows *are* mere formalities and nice words to many who get married. To non-Christians, they are merely promises. About the only thing that can be said to two people, sincere as they might be at the moment, is "Good luck. We wish you the best." Nothing more can be said. But to two Christians who have invited God, first into their personal lives as Lord and Savior, and then into their marriage, we can freely say, "The Lord bless and keep you."

The vows they take are taken in the presence of God and their families. The vows mean permanence. The vows bring down upon the two people making them God's blessing, power, and grace. God promises, as a participant in the covenant, to energize, sustain, and guide the marriage.

*Rings are exchanged.* All covenants have a sign or seal. When God entered into covenant with Noah and his household, he sealed it with the rainbow. When God entered into covenant with Abraham and his household, he sealed it with circumcision. When a man and woman enter into a sacred covenant, they seal it with a ring. It is the visible reminder, the sign that sacred vows have been taken in the presence of God. Thus, the words are spoken, "I give you this ring, as a sign of my promise, in the name of the Father, the Son, and the Holy Spirit," or, "With this ring, I thee wed."

*A prayer is offered and blessing given.* If God is not involved in the marriage, if the two being married have not committed themselves to God in their own private lives, what is there to pray about? But when two Christians are being married and have entered into a covenant by sacred vow, God is asked to bless them and to make them one flesh.

## MARRIAGE AND PARENTS

Marriage springs from the covenant relationships in which the husband and wife were raised. Their parents offered them when infants by sacred vow to God. It signifies the blessing that passes from parent to child, from one generation to the next (Genesis 17:1-14).

Because the family is a covenant relationship, what involvement should fathers and mothers have in approving and blessing the marriages of their children? If the marriage ceremony signifies the passing of the priestly responsibilities from father to groom, and from father to son, should they also be involved in the process, in the prayers, in the decisions?

- Sociologists have noted that the culture in which the decision about marriage is confined solely to the two being married, is the culture with the highest rate of marriage failure and divorce.

- Christian counselors indicate that when they encounter marriages that are in trouble, they have learned to ask two preliminary questions. First, did you together violate God's law prior to marriage through sexual impurity? If so, have you together before God repented of that, talked about it, and asked each other for forgiveness? Second, did you marry in violation of the counsel of your parents, and, thus, without their blessing? If so, have you asked their forgiveness? (If you would not think of driving away with your bride's father's car without his permission, why would you presume that you could take his daughter in marriage without his permission?)

## BIG IDEAS OF THIS TAPE:

1. Christian marriage is not merely a contract confirmed with a promise, but is a *covenant* sealed by a sacred vow.
2. The sacred vow is taken with *God* as witness.

3. The marriage covenant can be entered into only with another *Christian*.

4. By sacred vow each person gives not *property* but *person* to the other.

5. The sacred vow of the marriage covenant is a commitment for *life*.

6. By sacred vow each person commits to becoming an instrument in God's hands for the perfecting in godliness of the other.

7. All of the major components of the Christian marriage ceremony point to the centrality of the fact of marriage as *covenant*.

8. Marriage as covenant involves not only two persons, but also two entire *families*.

## FINAL NOTE:

Nothing can require more of us by way of commitment, energy, planning, prayer, time, or concentration than the marriage covenant. It is higher in importance than vocation, more demanding than play and recreation, and is more necessary than church involvement or any other activity or relationship. It is central to God's earthly program.

Preparing for the marriage covenant is more important than college training, military training, or vocational training.

There is no higher calling, no more important commitment, and no greater responsibility. Christian marriage is nobler than royalty, worthier than being president of a country, and more desirable than the highest position in a leading company.

Prayerfully prepare yourself for it well.

## QUESTIONS FOR FURTHER THOUGHT AND DISCUSSION

1. How has the confusion between marriage as contract and marriage as covenant caused disruption in our society and culture?

2. Which is more important, the marriage license or the marriage covenant? Why?

3. Are two persons who are deeply in love, who desire to be married, and who are secular in their life attitudes and life allegiances, able to enter into marriage as a covenant? Why, or why not? What aspect of the marriage covenant would create a major problem for them? Why?

4. Why is it impossible and fatal for a Christian to attempt entering into a marriage covenant with a non-Christian?

5. Explore the biblical passage, Malachi 2:10-16. How does it support the big ideas of this tape? Explain what each item means in your own words.

6. In the same biblical passage, what does it say about God's attitude towards divorce? How does this coincide with what Jesus said in Matthew 19:3-6?

7. Why, in the light of the big ideas of this chapter, is preparation prior to marriage so important?

8. What do you think would be important items to concentrate on in preparation for marriage? Which could be thought about and developed prior to actually meeting the person you will marry? Which would better be developed during your engagement to the person you will marry?

9. What will you have to be as a person in order to adequately carry out your part of a marriage covenant? What qualities, abilities, and personal attributes are necessary?

10. What will another person have to be in order to adequately carry out their part of a marriage covenant they enter with you? What qualities, abilities, and personal attributes are necessary?